D1706499

Sam Fuller : Film Is a Battleground

Sam Fuller
Film Is a Battleground

A Critical Study, with Interviews,
a Filmography and a Bibliography

by LEE SERVER

McFarland & Company, Inc., Publishers
Jefferson, North Carolina, and London

British Library Cataloguing-in-Publication data are available

Library of Congress Cataloguing-in-Publication Data

Server, Lee.
    Sam Fuller : film is a battleground : a critical study, with
interviews, a filmography and a bibliography / by Lee Server.
        p.   cm.
    Includes bibliographical references and index. ∞
    ISBN 0-7864-0008-0 (lib. bdg.: 50# alk. paper)
    1. Fuller, Samuel, 1912-   — Criticism and interpretation.
I. Title.
PN1998.3.F85S47   1994
791.43′0233′092 — dc20
[B]   94-10983
                                                              CIP

©1994 Lee Server. All rights reserved

Manufactured in the United States of America

McFarland & Company, Inc., Publishers
    Box 611, Jefferson, North Carolina 28640

for Terri

Acknowledgments

I am indebted to the generous contributions and encouragement of a number of people. First and foremost I wish to thank Sam Fuller and Christa Lang Fuller for hours of hospitality and enthusiastic conversation in Paris. I am also grateful to Sam's associates and admirers who agreed to talk with me: Gene Evans, the late Vincent Price, Richard Widmark, Robert Stack, Constance Towers, Joseph Biroc, Stanley Cortez, Adam Greenberg, Bruce Surtees, Gene Fowler, Jr., Karl Lewis Miller, Larry Cohen and Gene Corman.

A number of other individuals and organizations aided in the completion of this project and must be thanked: Dean Server; Terry Geesken and Mary Corliss at the Museum of Modern Art; Bruce Goldstein and Film Forum; the staff at the library of the Academy of Motion Picture Arts and Sciences; Bill Cunningham at *Variety*; Jerry Ohlinger's Movie Material Store; Larry Edmonds Bookshop; and in Paris, Cinedoc and Atmosphere.

Contents

"A film is like a battleground—love ... hate ...
action ... violence ... death ... in one word—
emotion!"
— Samuel Fuller in Jean-Luc
Godard's *Pierrot le Fou*

Visions! omens! hallucinations! miracles!
ecstasies! down the American river!
— from *Howl* by Allen Ginsberg

Introduction

Samuel Michael Fuller, of Park Row, Hollywood and Paris, is a singular figure in the history of motion pictures. A tabloid poet, a formal innovator, a radical individualist, he is the writer-director of twenty-three of the most original, eccentric, and explosive movies ever made. His filmography is a unique paradox: work born for the most part in the lower depths of the "B" movie mills, yet shot through with elements seldom seen outside the rarefied worlds of the avant-garde and "art" film: autobiography, thematic obsessions and technical experimentation. From his directorial debut, the 1949 "non–Western" *I Shot Jesse James,* to the European-produced *Street of No Return,* released in 1989, Fuller has transcended the limitations imposed by laughably meager budgets, 10-day shooting schedules, hackneyed genres and grind-house audiences. Each of his "yarns" — as he calls his stories of crime and lust and war — is a free-fire zone of the unexpected and audacious: Baroque compositions, long takes and elaborate camera movements; controversial and "shocking" subject matter; big themes and dangerous ones — race, politics, patriotism. Fuller takes a palpable pleasure in subverting Hollywood's clichés and standards of behavior. His protagonists are the sort most ambitious directors eschew, the dregs, lowlife criminals and hookers, stubbly-chinned dogfaces, borderline psychopaths and a few who cross the border and don't look back. Fuller hates the mainstream moviemakers' sanitized, idealized depictions of human behavior. When his characters get shot or stabbed or blown up there are no deathbed scenes or beatific last words, but screams of agony. If forced to choose between a fast buck and a noble gesture, they take the cash.

Examples of Fuller's raw iconoclasm are legion. In *Forty Guns* an escaping killer holds his sister — the film's leading lady — as a shield, daring the lawman hero to shoot and risk hitting her; the lawman shoots them both. In the famous cold opening of *The Naked Kiss,* a hand-held point-of-view shot, an enraged Constance Towers flails at the camera as her wig flies off to reveal a completely shaven head. In Fuller's most productive period, the 1950s, he confronted the pieties of a conformist Zeitgeist. In *The Steel Helmet,* his GI hero loses his temper and murders a prisoner of war. The U.S. Army and

1

various right-wing columnists were outraged. In *Pickup on South Street*, Richard Widmark's cocky three-time-loser pickpocket, preparing to sell government secrets to the highest bidder, ridicules the patriotic appeals of a righteous FBI agent. Asked if he knows what treason means, Widmark sneers, "Who cares!" J. Edgar Hoover was mortified.

And Fuller's talent to enrage was not confined to the rigid spirit of the McCarthy era—in the jaded 1980s, by then a grand old man of the cinema, Fuller could still drive people crazy. His film *White Dog* was so embroiled in controversy that the studio felt forced to cancel its release. While Hollywood occasionally allowed itself to make a heartfelt or sanctimonious "problem picture," serious subject matter was taboo in escapist genre fare. Fuller, eagerly breaking the rules, infused his action pictures with just such controversial elements to create war movies, gangster movies, Westerns and police whodunits that deal with bigotry, interracial romance, sexual hysteria, mental illness. Similarly, Fuller has always sought to break away from Hollywood's stylistic constraints. Long before the French New Wave liberated film grammar from conservative and paralyzing self-effacement—the master shot/two-shot, unobtrusive cutting and camera movement style of commercial filmmaking—Fuller was making movies full of anarchically unconstrained cinematic effects, reel-length takes, complex camera movements and vertiginous angles, Pudovkinlike montages, shock cuts and concussive closeups.

From his first film, Fuller made it clear he would not be working in the big studio mode of anonymous craftsmanship. He used the camera and the moviola like noisy weapons. When Fuller has something on his mind his characters confront it head-on with loquacious didacticism. He writes scenes and dialogue directly from his own personal experiences and fills the edges of each film with autobiographical details—recurring names and places from his past, photos of friends and heroes, copies of his books, posters and props from his movies and assorted other iconographic material ranging from military insignias to cigars. No auteurist phrenology is needed to determine Fuller's influence on his work. Alone among Hollywood directors, Fuller has written or co-written the scripts of all of his films, produced most of them, and even financed one—*Park Row*—solely from his own pocket, maintaining a highly personal cinematic vision for more than four decades. Like him or loathe him—and there are more than a handful who would find his work crude, pretentious or plain weird—few would deny Fuller his unique status in the American cinema.

There are two formative influences on Sam Fuller's life and career: war and journalism. His extensive combat experience as an infantryman in World War II, including his Omaha Beach landing on D-Day, gave him the knowledge and the determination to make an authentically detailed, unsentimentalized war movie when he returned to Hollywood. Rarely, he felt, had the movies captured anything like the mix of horror, banality and nihilism

Sam Fuller directing *The Big Red One* (1980).

of actual combat. In a long letter to Lewis Milestone, director of *All Quiet on the Western Front*, in 1946, Fuller, respectfully angry, went on at length about the phoniness of Milestone's latest war film, *A Walk in the Sun*. "Why a man of your calibre," Fuller wrote, "should resort to a colonel's technical advice on what happens to a platoon is something I'll never figure out. . . . When colonels are back in their garrison hutments where they belong I'll come out with a yarn that won't make any doggie that was ever on the line retch with disgust." And he concludes, "Some day there'll be an *All Quiet on the American doggie* and I'm going to do my best to be the doggie to write it."

Fuller's chance came with the third film he directed, *The Steel Helmet*. His hope to capture the reality of war may have been contained by a minuscule budget and a phony soundstage setting, but Fuller invested his meager production with so much dogface detail, iconoclastic behavior and forceful violence that the film was a sensation, stirring up controversy and making a fortune. Fuller's subsequent war films continued to show his anti-cliché attitude and illustrate his philosophy, stated in *The Big Red One*, that "the only glory in war is survival." Of course, Fuller's obsession with war and the military is felt in the non-war films as well. Various civilians are seen to have had their character made or destroyed by combat experience. Friendships formed "in a foxhole" tie people together for life. The gangsters in *House of Bamboo* and *Underworld USA* are said to run their criminal enterprises exactly like military operations. Life, in Fuller films, is often just a large-scale, unending version of war. "Love," says Mac, the cigar-smoking female artist in *The Crimson Kimono*, "is like a battleground ... somebody has to get a bloody nose." And Fuller returns to the analogy for his cameo appearance in Godard's *Pierrot le Fou*, defining the cinema for Jean Paul Belmondo.

Journalism is Fuller's lifelong love. Of his old livelihood he has said (with a nice combination of the sentimental and the mercenary), "If only a reporter could get a thousand dollars an hour the way a director can, I'd be in it today." A very young crime reporter in New York in the 1920s, Fuller was a junior contemporary of all those Prohibition Era newshawks who went to Hollywood when sound came in: Hecht and MacArthur, Herman Mankiewicz, Gene Fowler, Rian James, Allen Rivkin, Courtney Terrett, and others, who set the tough, cynical, wisecracking, newspaper-bred tone for countless golden age movies. New York in the 1920s was the heyday of the tabloids, sensationalized, picture-heavy, lowest-common-denominator "rags," often pitched against each other in outrageous circulation wars. Fuller wrote his first stories at the most outrageous tabloid of them all, the *Graphic*. The brainchild of crackpot publisher (and America's premiere vegetarian) Bernarr Macfadden, and Fulton Oursler, future author of *The Greatest Story Ever Told* ("The only man," said an envious associate, "who would plagiarize the Holy Bible and make money off it"), the *Graphic* took New York by storm with its mixture of tawdry scandals, crusades for the common man, contests and bizarre promotional stunts, all topped off by a daily screaming headline: "Professors Held in Co-ed Hammer Slaying," "Vice Girl's Arm Broken in Brutal Police Raid," "Society Dames Neck Negroes," "Sinclair Lewis Socked by Dreiser." The *Graphic* had the motto "Nothing But the Truth," but its definition of the truth was idiosyncratic at best. The paper pioneered the use of a photo lab technique called the "Composograph," which involved the faking of news photographs with a double exposure process. This allowed the paper to print circulation-boosting pictures of executions and celebrity "love nests" that would otherwise not exist. *Graphic* staffers, including Sam Fuller, often doubled for the characters being "photographed," and the staged hanging of killer Gerald Chapman nearly cost the life of the copy boy pretending to be Chapman. The public went wild for the paper's heady brew of sex, scandal and ultraviolence, although bluenoses of the period and bitter journalistic rivals dubbed it the *Porno-Graphic*.

It was in this atmosphere that Fuller learned to tell stories, and the *Graphic*'s guiding "principle" of "creative exaggeration," as well as its emphasis on the sanguinary nightmare side of American life, obviously exerted a strong influence on the tough, hyperbolic, sometimes shocking films Fuller would write and direct. He has often said that his dream would be to publish and edit his own newspaper, and, besides those works that deal directly with journalism (*Park Row, Shock Corridor,* the scripts or stories for *Confirm or Deny, Power of the Press, Scandal Sheet*), all of Fuller's films can be viewed in newspaper terms, with their abundance of graphics (headlines, mottoes, epigraphs, datelines, etc.), the "front page" premises, war reporting, exposés, didactic editorials, investigative journalism, and perhaps a bit of the bluntness of the "funny pages."

Of course, in the 1930s, unlike today, the connection between journalism and the movies was considered a natural one, and Fuller, like hundreds of other reporters, was eventually lured to Hollywood to write screenplays. His name appeared on screen no fewer than eight times during this first period in the movie capital, but the obscure programmers he contributed to did nothing to secure his future. It was not until his return after World War II, with a successful novel—*The Dark Page*—under his belt and a film rights sale to Howard Hawks, that Fuller began to get the big studios' attention. His frustration with the producer/committee system at the studios led Fuller to make a deal to write and direct a film, without interference, for a minor independent producer named Robert Lippert. That first film, *I Shot Jesse James,* with its "headline" title, made money and Fuller did two more films for Lippert. The third one, *The Steel Helmet,* was the sleeper of its year, a quirky and unexpectedly entertaining film with front page timeliness in its Korean War setting.

Fuller made a fortune from his piece of the film, was wooed by all the studios, and entered a lengthy relationship with 20th Century–Fox. Perhaps in hiring the tough-talking ex-GI, Darryl Zanuck thought he was getting a new action-specialist workhorse along the lines of Fox veteran Henry Hathaway. In fact, Fuller's idiosyncratic artistry was closer to that of the studio's two carriage-trade contractees—emotionally explosive Elia Kazan and talkative, didactic Joseph Mankiewicz. In any case, Fuller adjusted his wild streak for the more genteel needs of the big studio, and turned out a series of excellent entertainments in an assortment of genres—*Pickup on South Street, House of Bamboo, Forty Guns, Fixed Bayonets.* By all accounts Fuller and studio chief Darryl Zanuck got on like gangbusters, the mogul apparently taking great pleasure in Fuller's hardboiled personality and theatricality. Producer and screenwriter Philip Dunne recalled for me a meeting in Zanuck's office that was interrupted by an explosion. "You could hear what sounded like a bomb going off and all the windows rattled. Darryl looked off into the distance and smiled and just said, 'That's Sammy Fuller blowing the ass out of Stage 16. . .' Sammy had a violent streak and Darryl enjoyed it very much."

Zanuck withdrew as production head in the late 1950s, and Fuller moved on to other studios and made several films for his own production company, Globe Enterprises (named after the crusading newspaper he invented for *Park Row*). Fuller's films remained in the "B" or "A – " category; a single production, *Merrill's Marauders*, showed the sort of epic visual effects Fuller could achieve with a big budget. By the early 1960s, with *Shock Corridor* and *The Naked Kiss*, he had come full circle, back to extremely low-cost independent filmmaking on the far fringes of Hollywood. These two films, original and in many ways brilliant works, became a kind of professional dead end. Fuller found great difficulties in getting other projects off the ground. A Mexican adventure movie, *Shark*, became an almost unreleasable mess (Fuller disowns the picture), and Fuller's next film, a confused and self-conscious thriller made in Germany, *Dead Pigeon on Beethoven Street*, was another setback for the writer-director.

Ironically, as Fuller's career seemed to become permanently derailed, his status among critics, film buffs and young filmmakers, was skyrocketing. In the late 1950s he had been "discovered" by the French critics at *Cahiers du Cinéma*. Not beholden to the class-consciousness of the Anglo-American critical community, the *Cahiers* writers were stunned by Fuller's visionary work within the "B" movie, drive-in ghetto. Jean-Luc Godard rhapsodized over *Forty Guns*: "So rich in invention and bursting with daring conceptions that it reminds one of the extravagances of Abel Gance and Stroheim." Godard in particular was impressed by Fuller's radical style, the didacticism and frenzied, experimental technique. Through Godard, when the critic turned filmmaker, Fuller would influence the entire modernist movement in the cinema of the 1960s. By the 1970s, Fuller had been lionized by practically every film festival, archive, and museum in the world. But in Hollywood he remained unemployed.

At the end of the decade, he had finally staged a "comeback." After many delays and revised ambitions, Fuller was able to complete a dream project, *The Big Red One*, the largely autobiographical epic of an infantry outfit in World War II, a story that would travel from North Africa to Omaha Beach and on to the concentration camp at Falkenau, just as foot soldier Sam Fuller had done thirty-some years before. His comeback picture brought affectionate tributes from mainstream publications, including profiles in *Newsweek* and the Sunday *New York Times*. As his followup to *The Big Red One*, Fuller chose to make *White Dog*, an unusual project offered to him by Paramount. The resulting film was brilliant and characteristic, a thought-provoking thriller on a controversial subject. Protesters attacked the film as racist before it was even completed. Although the charges were groundless — the film is ferociously anti-racist — the studio panicked and the movie was shelved. Fuller, stung by the turn of events, accepted an offer to make a film in France (*Les Voleurs de la nuit*, released in 1982) and he has lived in Paris ever since. In 1988 he co-wrote and directed *Street of No Return*, from the novel by David Goodis, another celebrated American name in France. Shot in Lisbon, Portugal, on stylized locations of a haunting emptiness, *Street* was a stunning film noir about love and memory and revenge, full of visual poetry and manic energy.

Nearing the age of eighty, Fuller remained, undiminished, a great and unique filmmaker.

Interview
with Sam Fuller

Sam Fuller has lived in Paris since the early 1980s. He does not consider himself an exile — his house and swimming pool are still waiting for him in the hills above Hollywood — but his last three films all emanated from his Paris base, and his professional connections are now largely within the European film community of admiring young producers, directors and cinéastes. Paris is a good place to live if you are a legendary Hollywood filmmaker. The city is movie mad, with its hundreds of theaters, a hefty percentage of them screening revivals from every era, and film books on the most esoteric *auteurs* in every drugstore and train station. Fuller, with his fierce, outlandish movies and personality, is a genuine celebrity in France, an American icon.

His Paris home is on a prosperous residential street in the 8th *arrondissement*. He lives with his wife, the actress Christa Lang (seen in Godard's *Alphaville* and the star of Fuller's own *Dead Pigeon on Beethoven Street*), and their daughter, Samantha. Christa is fluent in several languages and Samantha is bilingual; Sam speaks *American*. Their centuries-old apartment is elegantly peeling around the edges. The large, high-ceilinged rooms show few signs of Fuller's occupancy — only a French poster for 20th Century–Fox, his former studio, and a cluttered work space where various scripts and loose pages of notes surround a battered steel typewriter that looks like it was manufactured around the time *The Front Page* opened on Broadway.

In old age, Fuller is small-framed and white-haired, but possessed of a violent energy and enthusiasm. He stormed Omaha Beach on D-Day, 1944, and he looks like he could do it again tomorrow. An interview is a performance, a one-man Sam Fuller movie, as he paces the floor, spitting out anecdotes in a Ned Sparks–like side-of-the-mouth snarl, punctuated by frequent bursts of Homeric laughter and an imperial wave of the ever-present cigar (dark leaf Comacho Number One, when available). A printed transcript can never do justice to the exuberant melodrama of Fuller in conversation.

The interview that follows has been edited to the extent that a few

9

sections have been shifted to fit a chronological order, and I have cut several long tangential discussions of current affairs and recent film releases. I have also greatly reduced the number of my own verbatim comments and inter-jections to give Fuller's responses greater continuity.

Most of what follows comes from a single marathon session in the Paris apartment, one overcast Sunday in October. It began in the early afternoon and lasted through dinner and late into the night, long after I had run out of recording tape and questions.

Let's begin at the beginning—

Before we go any farther you might as well get at least one fact straight. They always put a year on my age. I was born in 1912. Some nuthead in France wrote me down a long time ago as born in 1911 and lazy writers have kept repeating it ever since.

Nineteen twelve then. We come from the same neck of the woods. I'm from Springfield. You grew up in Worcester.

Worcester. Worcester, Massachusetts. A fucking dull town and we left when I was eleven. My father died and we left—my mother, my brothers and me—for New York City. Now there was a city. Hoo! Nowhere like it on earth. New York City in the 1920s.

And you started working for the newspapers right away?

Peddling papers. Every kid sold papers in New York. There were eleven daily newspapers in New York then. Can you imagine that? Would have been a dream for a guy like you. Ha! Security. With eleven papers in town there had to be one where you'd fit in, that would like your mind and style. Ten editors in a row could hate you and you'd still have a job.

In those days the newsboys had to go to the circulation department and buy their papers. You bought a paper for a penny and sold it for two cents. Or you bought it for a penny-and-a-half and sold it for three. The *News* was two cents, the *Mirror* was two cents, the *Journal* was three cents. I would make about a dollar a day. You go to school in the daytime, get out at 2:15, take a subway—not getting lost, like certain people I know—and you got off at Park Place. You walked across City Hall Park, a short cut through the municipal building, and the goddamned windows and the Roman columns would knock you on your ass. Off Park Row, near the Bowery and China-town. Two Thirty-Eight William Street, at the foot of the Brooklyn Bridge. The *New York Evening Journal*. I fell in love with the *Journal*.

Did you stand on the street corner and shout the headline and "Extra!" like in old movies?

Of course! I'll give you something I never discussed with anyone. No one ever asked me about headlines before. I never was in the city room, but I got to know some of the newsmen outside. They would come out of the building, down the ramp on the side street and I got talking to a few of them. One time, a reporter stopped to talk with me. I was a kid, twelve and a half, thirteen. I didn't even know what he did on the paper, but he was a reporter, and he said, "Look, why don't you, if you want to really yell a headline, there's a good story here." A story he had written for the *Journal*. "See that story, young fella?" An insane man had raped a woman and escaped. He was out of a mental hospital and he raped someone and escaped. This reporter says, "I'll write something for you and you yell it." And I did it, I yelled the headline: "NUT SCREWS... BOLTS!"

Now there was a man named O. O. McIntyre who was on the *Daily American*. He wrote a column every day, a lovely column about New York, page one every morning. Not a gossip column. And he wrote a little item about me, the newsboy shouting the headline, "NUT SCREWS, BOLTS... READ ALL ABOUT IT!" I didn't even see it, but that same reporter after a couple of days saw me and gave me the clipping. He says, "Look, you're in the paper."

Then I got to know Tom Foley, the foreman at the two Hearst papers. The *Journal* in the evening and the *American* in the morning. Two papers, everything separated, but on the same floor. Foley had one eye and he was half-deaf. He took me up to the press room and I fell in love with that. It was Wonderland. He showed me the composing room, the Linotypes in action. And he took me to the editorial department. I finally got into the center of it all, the City Room, seventh floor.

From that moment I was done with peddling papers. I had to get a job inside the building. A job on the *Journal*. I saw boys, seventeen, eighteen years old, a little older than me, running around. Someone would call "Boy! Copy!" and they'd take something from one desk and run it over to another desk or shoot it down these pneumatic tubes. I asked what that was about and how could I get one of those jobs? I said to Tom Foley, "Who's the man to see?" And Foley says, "You talk to Joseph Mulcahy, he's the managing editor. He's the boss."

Joseph Mulcahy, the czar! When he breathed fire, people died. And I went to see him. He said, "How old are you?" I was about thirteen. He said, "You can't work. You've got to be fourteen or over and have working papers to work in New York City. Where you from?" I said, "Massachusetts." He says, "Don't they have working papers there?" I said, "No, I sold papers there." He says, "That's different. When you're a newsboy, you are your own boss. You are a capitalist."

But he told me the man to see about getting working papers, and told me to lie about my age. And he put me to work as a copy boy. I was there for two years and worked my way up, ended up getting the job as personal copy boy for the biggest and smartest editor in the U.S.A. — Arthur Brisbane.

The editor of thirty-four daily Hearst newspapers in thirty-four capitals in the
United States. With any one of those newspapers Hearst would have been
a powerful man. With one, you and I could retire happy. He had thirty-four.
And I'm not talking about his magazines, and radio and real estate. This was
the real Citizen Kane.

But Arthur Brisbane was the number one editorial writer in the world.
He had been with Pulitzer and had some fight with Pulitzer and Hearst nailed
him. That's a part of *Citizen Kane* that's very accurate, when he grabbed the
cream from the rival paper.

I went around with Brisbane every day, taking his copy. He had a dic-
taphone, and would dictate onto a wax disc in the back of his car—a Pierce
Arrow. And he would hold the little horn and dictate his column. Page one,
column one: "Today by Arthur Brisbane." And when he would finish a cylinder he would stop the car, wherever he was, and I would get out to take the
cylinder back to the paper. And he would always give me a dollar to take the
subway. But as soon as I saw his back turned—"*taxi!*" And you'd get into the
taxi and say, "*Journal.*" That's all you had to say. Not another word. Whew!
That taxi took off.

One time I was with him at Hearst's place on Riverside Drive. He had
two floors in an apartment building he owned, where he stayed when he was
in New York with his mistress, Marion Davies. And it was a party, people in
costumes, the most important people in the city were there. And there was
a butler in a real butler's outfit and I thought he was in another costume for
the party. And Mr. Brisbane met me in the kitchen—I never saw such a kitchen. Everything was pushbutton. Push button stoves, shelves. And Mr.
Brisbane ordered a chicken for me and put it in a bag, but there was oil and
grease coming out and he put it in two more bags so it wouldn't get on my
suit. And he said, "You take that home to your mother when you finish work.
And don't tell anybody in the City Room that you've got a chicken." I said,
"At the *Journal?* Nobody there would eat my chicken." But he was right and
I was wrong. The reporters found that chicken and ate it.

I worked for Brisbane for two and a half years. I was going on seventeen
and I wanted a job as a police reporter. He said no, forget it. He said, "Twenty-
one I'll put you on the street, not before. Not in this city." It was the time
of the bootleggers, gangsters, all that crap. I wanted to cover it. Crime! So I
got an offer to go work for another paper called the *New York Evening
Graphic,* owned by Bernarr McFadden. They promised me a couple dollars
a week raise to be their head copy boy, and the managing editor, a man named
Emile Gauvreau, promised to make me a reporter. I told Brisbane. I said, "I'm
going to the *Graphic.*" It was a new paper and pretty much of a scandal paper.
And he said, "It won't last long, that paper. You'll regret it."

But the *Graphic* was a sensation. And Gauvreau kept his promise and
made me a crime reporter. I was seventeen.

The Graphic *indulged in yellow journalism, to say the least.*
"Creative exaggeration."

The paper would fake photos of disasters or the latest scandal.
I posed for some of them. We did a composite of two French aviators who had crashed in the mid–Atlantic. My mother couldn't understand it. She wanted to know, if we got that close to them with our photographer why we couldn't have saved them.

As a teenaged crime reporter you must have been competing against some very experienced men.
I was scared. I was scared about that word, "scoop." I was tense. I wanted to get things that the older men didn't, and they knew that. My first assignment, my first real assignment, was a double hit—a murder and a suicide. My editor, Emile Gauvreau, said, "This is a little ticklish. A man and his mistress. It's going to be your story, I want you on it, but I want you to have someone who will show you the ropes." At the *Graphic* we had three women, top women reporters. One was Rhea Gore—John Huston's mother, Walter Huston's ex-wife—a wonderful woman. She broke me in as a newspaper crime reporter. I went on several stories then with her and she really showed me things, shortcuts.

A police reporter would stay close to police headquarters on Center Street or at a police precinct. My first precinct was Forty-Seventh Street, the Tenderloin of New York. Across the street from the precinct was a plumber's shop. And in the back room of the plumber's shop was the press room. There's five or six or eight phones in the back room of that plumber shop—you're not allowed to use the police station for that work—and all the papers rented that back room. You picked up your phone and flipped a key, it's an outside line, on another key it's a direct line to your editor. I only phoned a story in if I was working against the clock. The leeway was an hour and a half to two hours before lockup in the press room. If you couldn't make that you phoned it to "rewrite." Otherwise, what you do, as soon as you got your facts you run down to the paper and write it. They could change it, blue pencil anything they wanted, or ask for more, but you wrote it. And I covered everything: murders, executions, leapers, race riots. Grisly things. But I didn't look at it in that way as a young reporter. I couldn't worry about blood, I was afraid I would miss a name, miss an address, miss out on something very important to the desk, to the paper.

Police corruption was rampant, from all reports. Did you have respect for the police or were they your antagonists on the way to a story?
Respect? Yes and no. Some were very good. They were doing a job as best they could. And some were out to get all they could.

What about the "third degree," police beating confessions out of suspects?

Of course! Listen, the people expect too much of the police. Go to New York City and check on the homicide files. You'll see they are very difficult to solve. Read your Sherlock Holmes and the others, working out the different progressive steps—it's not the butler, it's not the wench, it's not the Pope, look, there's the clue behind the radiator! But that's not *real*. In real life, a real murder is very seldom solved. You don't find a thumbprint and bring in the killer. It's not the way it is in murder mysteries, *The Thin Man*, the Chandler series—*wonderful* books, but it's not real! To solve a crime you need a confession or an informant or a double-crossed wench...

Look, your girlfriend robbed a bank with you, you got away with a million bucks or five hundred dollars, whatever it was. You lay low, nobody catches you. Then you go for another girl. You give the old girl some money, tell her to go to hell. She goes for the phone. "Spring, 3-1000." "Police head-quarters." She says, "Homicide." She says, "Go to the Olympia Hotel. Room 412. Lee Server. Held up the Phoenix National Bank two years ago, killed three men." Bang! she hangs up the phone. And next day the police say it was their long hours of research and investigation.

I've been around a lot of police stations. Police stations, the city morgue. That was my beat and I loved it.

Emile Gauvreau is a legendary figure from that period. What can you tell me about him?

Gauvreau was editor of the *Graphic*, and many books and films have been based on him. What he did with a killer in Connecticut was exactly the situation they used in *The Front Page* where the murderer is hidden in the desk. Gauvreau hid his killer in the city room, questioned him, got the story written and waited till the paper was on the street before he handed him over to the police.

That's when he had to get out of Hartford and went to New York and Macfadden gave him the job. I was at the opening night of *The Front Page*. Me and a reporter from the *Daily News*. We watched Lee Tracy and that was the reporter we wanted to be.

Gauvreau was the model for the editor in Five Star Final, *right?*

That is correct. *Five Star Final*—Edward G. Robinson played the editor in the movie—was factual. It was written by Louis Weitzenkorn. Weitzen-korn replaced Gauvreau when Gauvreau went to the *Mirror*, following Walter Winchell, who hated him. For *Five Star Final* he used one of Gauvreau's exploits. He revived an old murder case, publishing the murder-ess's name and address, which led to the suicide of the woman and her husband. The play was very factual. I know because I was there and was involved in a very small way—I was sent to dig up facts about the woman's son (it became a daughter in the film). Weitzenkorn even used Gauvreau's habit of washing his hands when he felt guilty over a dirty story.

Did you get many scoops?

I broke the death of Jeanne Eagles. She was before your time, means nothing to you — she was the top actress on Broadway. Kim Novak played her in the movies. She died of a heroin overdose. I got a tip and found her corpse at Campbell's Funeral Parlor.

My biggest story, headlines for days, occurred just by chance. I was taking a walk with a cop in the Twenty-Fourth Precinct. He was transferred for the one night because another cop was sick. I knew him when he was a rookie and he was still a very young cop. We had a bite at the Horn and Hardart Automat and then we're walking. He got a call, a box call. That's a little red box that rings and only a cop has a key to open it up. That was the precinct calling for the cop in that vicinity. That's how they reached a cop on the beat. Or if there was trouble, the cops had billy clubs made of lead. They'd bang the pavement and it would make a bell ring that would shoot down the street and could be heard for a helluva long distance. So this cop, Edward Kane, got a call saying there was an argument between some people. A woman had called and reported a fight going on and gave the address: 45 Allen Street.

We're walking fast and he says, "There's something funny about this." This section was old warehouses and offices from the turn of the century, some goddamned buildings from the Boss Tweed days and the Civil War. There was no one living there. I say, "You're goddamned right there's something funny." And we got to 45 Allen Street. An office building, empty. And he says, "Let's try and get inside. Maybe someone lives in the building, maybe there's a clerk or a nightwatchman." So we went around and downstairs and tried to open a door. It could only open this much — something blocking it. We pushed it open and on the floor was a dead man.

We couldn't see much of it but we reached down and felt it. When our eyes adjusted and we could see a little better — there was only a dim incandescent light on — we saw the other body. It was an old man, an octogenarian, eighty-six, eighty-seven years old. He was grinning. It was Edward Ridley, a multi-millionaire and notorious miser well-known for foreclosing more mortgages than anyone in the history of New York. The other man was his young secretary. The secretary had been shot. The old man's head was bashed in with an old bookkeeper's stool. But there was no gun. Two people there and they are both dead.

The old man had twenty-four million dollars in the bank and he left it all to the secretary. But there's a law that says, if I die I can leave you money. But if you die first and then I die, I cannot leave you that money. And the forensic expert found that the deaths were simultaneous, or, at least, it was a question who the hell died first.

So we were there with the bodies and I said to the cop, "Give me ten minutes to get a guy to take a goddamned picture." He says, "For Christ sake, are you kidding? What am I going to say to the Captain?" I said, "I was with you when you came in here." So we made a deal and I got my pictures and a page one byline on it. My head was "WHO KILLED SANTA CLAUS?" Edward Ridley foreclosed most of his mortgages on Christmas. The murders were not solved, and the city offered twenty-five thousand dollars reward for anyone who could solve the crime. I stayed with the investigation and had page one for the third, fourth, fifth day. And that was the story that got me connected with the movies for the first time. But it was aborted. I got a call from MGM on Broadway. "Would you please have a meeting here with us?" And the fellow from MGM says, "I'll give you five thousand dollars to write up this story and give us a solution to the murders." I said, "Five thousand? You must be crazy. The police department is offering twenty-five thousand dollars for information leading to the conviction of the killer." The MGM man said, "Shit, you don't have to solve it for real . . . *this is the movies!*" I was insulted. I didn't do it.

Tell me about those first novels you published . . . Test Tube Baby *and the others.*

Yes, I was a hack writer for Godwin, for Phoenix, for Hillman-Curl, publishing houses in New York. They would call up, wire any newspaper man and ask for fifty or seventy-five thousand words. They would pay a few hundred dollars. If you didn't have a title they'd give you one, and let's have the whole thing in three weeks.

I based *Test Tube Baby* on an interview I did with a Nobel Prize winner, Dr. Alexis Karral. He created and developed the synthetic heart. He got a lot of money for research from the government, but most of his funds came from Colonel Charles Lindbergh. I'm not a fan of his—he was a fascist for my money, but that's neither here nor there. So Dr. Karral told me about the ectogenetic child. I said, "What the hell does that mean?" And he explained that he was working on the theory of artificial insemination. He gave me all the information—the temperature inside the vagina of a woman was *so* important. And he explained that if he could get the right temperature and planted the sperm inside the woman's body, he would have an ectogenetic child—a "test tube baby." And so I wrote a book called *Test Tube Baby* and years later that was on the cover of every magazine, that expression. And I got a kick out of it. But the book was kind of childish, silly.

And another of my titles became an expression years later: *Burn, Baby Burn!* It became a war cry for the Black Panthers. My story had nothing to do with that. It was about the execution of a woman who was pregnant—was it wrong or right? Can you burn a woman with a baby inside her? And then there was one called *Make Up and Kiss,* exposing what I knew about the cosmetics companies. I wrote some others under phony names. If your city editor saw your name outside the office too often he'd want to know where the hell you got all the spare time.

You left the Graphic *finally and worked at papers across the country.*

I was working my way west. I'd get a job in Rochester, Chicago, sometimes two, three weeks, sometimes six months, San Francisco, San Diego, dailies, weeklies. I learned how they handled things differently in every region. Different biases, different hates and sympathies.

Was there any particular reason why you decided to leave New York when you did?

I had just left the morgue. My mother was very, very upset with me. I always stank of formaldehyde. She didn't like it. A lot of people feel that way. That smell, connected with death. We don't want to be connected with anyone dealing with death. No one has ever introduced me to a mortician in my whole life, not socially. Are you friendly with any undertakers?

Nope.

Well, they must be a clique all their own, don't you think? But it was the smell my mother objected to. And I saw a newsreel at a theatre across from police headquarters, a tennis championship in California. And my God, the boys were all in white, and the girls were in these little white shorts, everything so clean. And I came out of the theatre in New York and it was raining like hell. I said, "Fuck this." California!

What was the first thing you did for the movies?

I sold my first story while I was on a sheet. I sold a story about Dallas and Fort Worth—they both had expositions, centennials, and they were fighting, vying with each other, and my story had a New York fella take advantage of their petty jealousy. I sold this to a producer, it was a joke, really, but I gained a couple thousand dollars. I had never seen that much money. You didn't think about money when you worked on a newspaper. They paid you just enough to starve. But this story must have triggered this outfit, Republic Pictures, to track me down and call me. I was at the Morrison Hotel in Chicago. I had come to work on the *American.* They had no opening when I got there. I slept on a pool table my first night. And I got a call from someone at a studio called Republic. Did I have anything? I said, "Yes, sure." He said, "If you write it while I'm here, I'll pay you here." I said, "Look, did you ever hear of a man named Asbury, Herbert Asbury?" He said no. I said, "Well, he wrote a history of the gangs in my city, called *Gangs of New York,* and it's great. Now, my idea is you buy the book from him—I don't know if he's alive or dead—and I will take one little bit of that book. One piece out of a

hundred years of crime in America. And I'll turn that into a story for you."
And the man from Republic says, "Here's the money."

I wrote it in a day-and-a-half, just a story. And the guy from Republic
says, "I want you to come and work on a script." I said, "Gee, that's great. I'll
take off three or four weeks." So I went west. And I went to work on a script.
But Republic tried to double-cross me. They didn't want to pay for using the
book. I found out that you can't copyright a title—I didn't know that at the
time. And that made me ashamed of them.

I was writing script now and I didn't know what the hell I was working
on. It was all nonsense to me. But because of that I met a writer, a fine writer
with a big excellent name in Hollywood. And he had a blonde, beautiful
secretary and he was taking her to Hawaii or someplace. He had to have an
assigned script in by such a date. He told his wife he was going to Hawaii to
concentrate, to work on the script. And he said to me, "You write a screenplay for me, I pay you, we put my name on it." I said, "Of course!" He came
back from his trip, looked very haggard—his wife didn't think he was going
to last very long after that trip to Hawaii. And he liked my script. He told
another writer friend and before you know it a lot of guys were calling me
to ghost write. I became a ghost writer.

What was the name of the guy who went to Hawaii?
Never mind. I can't tell you. A very big name. And then there was a play
being written by someone, who I also shall not mention, and his agent con-
tacted me. This was Charles Feldman, the biggest agent in Hollywood. He
told me, it was subject matter the writer didn't know anything about. I didn't
know anything about it either. But he said, "Forget about it. Just do it. Write
what you can." I said okay and I did it. They put it on. Big star, big director,
big hit.

And then he began to call on me for a lot of different writers.

Still without credit?
That was the deal. I didn't want their fucking credit. I wanted the
money. I had a mother. Once in a while I'd sell a little yarn myself, but for
peanuts. The big money was when I put somebody else's name on it.

*But wasn't that because those writers already had some good credits behind
them?*
Of course, I found out. The studios respected past performance. If you
did write five successful screenplays, the producer will read your sixth
screenplay a helluva lot different than he will a screenplay by me. Sure. And
I did start to get credits. This was '37, '38. And I sold an original to 20th Century–Fox, under my own name, with a friend of mine, Hank Wales. Fritz
Lang wanted to make it and that's how I met Lang. The story was called

Fuller wrote the story and co-wrote the script for the 1937 Republic melodrama *Gangs of New York*, starring Charles Bickford.

Confirm or Deny. It's about a wire service, AP reporter, in London. Hitler's bombing, people living underground like gophers. They fucked around with it, and Lang walked off the picture after a week. He liked my story, but he didn't like the unrealistic bullshit they were putting in, romance and crap.

And then I was drafted. I was writing a book, *The Dark Page*, and ghosting for a director-producer, Otto Preminger. A wonderful guy. He paid me every week from his pocket. I went to the draft board and I said, "I can't get into a goddamned war yet." And the man says, "What do you mean, you can't?" I said, "I'm writing a book. And I have to write this and it has to make money." He said, "Is it a good book?" I said, "What's the difference?" I wrote a lot of books. Some are lousy. Who gives a goddamn. I said, "I think this is a good book." So he laughed and said, "How long will it take?" I said, "I don't know, two or three months." He said, "Okay. Finish it."

But I was afraid the call was coming so I raced it. It was a newspaper story, a psychological study of an editor who murders his wife. And I raced through the first draft and then they called. I'm drafted. They said, "We don't care now if it's finished or not." I said, "It's finished. Nothing you can do about it." And I told my mother, "I'm drafted. I don't know what they're going to do with me. They said I'll be gone maybe four, six months." I gave her my rough draft of *The Dark Page* and told her, "Don't do anything with it

Don Ameche and Joan Bennett in *Confirm or Deny* (1941), cowritten by Fuller.

because when I get back I'm really going to sit down and polish the goddamned thing." And the irony is that *she* sold it, I didn't. I was in North Africa, in a place that means nothing to you, near Tunisia. I got a letter from my mother. She did not say she sold my book, she said she *spent the advance* that Duell, Sloan & Pearce gave me for *The Dark Page.* I used that in *Big Red One,* but I called the book *Dark Deadline.*

I didn't get to see a copy of the printed book till I got to France, near St. Lo. Then, when I got to Germany, in the Hurtgen Forest, I got a long delayed letter and telegram from Charles Feldman, who became my agent. And he had sold *Dark Page* to Howard Hawks who wanted to make it a film with Bogart and Robinson. Hawks paid fifteen thousand dollars for the rights.

In what ways was your experience of war different from what you expected, or what someone who has only seen war in the movies might expect?

In the movies it is almost impossible to show a real war, to photograph battle. There is smoke everywhere. And the average moviegoer does not want to see real war. Not *real* war! Men afraid, men vomiting, men shitting in their pants, men shooting men on their own team. And *before* battle, there's no movie there. Before an invasion the soldier is sleeping. He's trying to sleep as much as he can because afterward he doesn't know when he'll get another chance.

You have said that the public image of the "war hero" is very inaccurate. Didn't you originally turn down John Wayne's offer to do "Big Red One" for that reason?

I could have had John Wayne, number one star in the world. He called me and we had lunch at the Polo Lounge in Beverly Hills. This was around 1960. He wanted to do it. But I couldn't. He was wrong for it. I don't care about his politics. But he is a symbol of a kind of man I never saw in war. He would have given it a *heroic* touch that I hate in war movies. In a real combat situation everyone is scared, everyone is a nervous animal. You can't determine the heroes from the cowards in advance. A lot of those John Wayne–type characters came through in combat and a lot of them fell apart. The ones you didn't expect anything from, you'd be surprised what they could do in that situation, when you're *cornered*. I saw things men did—they might have been called heroes later, but we didn't call them that. You were doing your job. Or you were saving your ass. If you got spotted—an officer has to be one of your witnesses—you got a medal. I got some. If you weren't spotted—nothing.

A lot of what happens on the battlefield is revised for public relations purposes, right? They simplify it, put a good spin on it . . .

They can't let the reality out. It would be a disaster. There are thousands of guys killed in battle and they don't even know their identity—they're blown up. An eyeball there, an arm here, a penis there—that's what you get on the battlefield. They scrape them up, throw them into a goddamn mattress cover, bury them. They're often reported MIA, Missing in Action. They're not, they're KIA. But they can't identify them and they don't want to take a chance of saying, "Your son Lee was killed in action" and then three days later you're alive. Jesus, your parents can sue the hell out of the government. The way their life was ruined. The way they became so depressed, or the father had a stroke because of the phrase KIA. So they say MIA, which means there's hope.

The dialogue in "Big Red One" about the insane asylum is very good on the things done strictly for "good p.r."

They're going to attack an insane asylum in Belgium and one guy says, "Why the hell do we have to attack them—let them drop a bomb. Throw a shell in there." And Marvin, my sergeant, says, "Well, that's bad for the image back home, you see. We can't kill insane people. That would make us look bad." And a kid says, "It's bad for us to kill insane people?" "It sure is." "But it's okay to kill sane people?" He says, "That's right." And that's war. That's the hypocrisy of it.

When I came back from war, the only real argument I had with my mother was over the dropping of the A-bomb in Japan. She couldn't understand. How in hell could we kill a hundred thousand people at one time? I called her a hypocrite and she blew her top. But I said what was the difference if one was killed at a time or a hundred thousand? To her that was bestial but to me it was very logical. Get the goddamned thing over with quickly—in another half a year, eight months, maybe you'd lose another five hundred thousand people.

Tell me something about your experiences on D-Day. You landed on Omaha Beach.

When we hit the beach we were told we would be off of there in less than a half hour. But somebody didn't tell the Germans up on the cliff. We were there for three hours.

You were pinned down all that time?

Machine gun and artillery fire. Blood floating in the water, bodies everywhere. The regimental commander, George Taylor, led us out of there. He stood up, said something fantastic. He said, "Two kinds of people are going to stay on this beach, the ones that are dead and the ones that are going to die. Now let's get the hell out of here!" And we went.

You've said that you never looked at the faces of the dead you passed, only their boots.

Yes. German boots were black, G.I. boots were brown.

You had a movie camera with you for much of the war, didn't you?

It was an old sixteen millimeter camera my mother sent me. You weren't supposed to have a camera like that, but nobody ever cared what you did. I shot a lot of stuff with it, when it wasn't broken.

What was the most interesting or exciting thing you filmed?

We were in a German town and I had gone into the cellar of a house with a couple of fellas. We were cold and wet and we had our boots and socks drying next to the stove. And I'm looking through a window and see a German coming towards us. I put the camera up there and let it run, while we're trying to get our socks and shoes back on. And somebody shot the German. We went out to him and he was dying. We gave him a cigarette. And he said something I used later in *Big Red One*. He kept saying, "All is kaput. All is kaput."

But the best shots I got with that camera were taken at the Falkenau concentration camp. My captain wanted a record of what happened there. I shot it all. The German officers loading the bodies of their victims onto wagons, pulling them through the town. My captain wanted these townspeople to see it, put their noses in it, to look at what they claimed they didn't know anything about. The camps, the ovens, the dead. I shot many reels of this stuff.

After the war you worked for a time with Howard Hawks. He had bought the film rights to The Dark Page.

Yeah. I was crazy about him.

He wanted you to write a script of The Sun Also Rises?

Wow, I was just going to tell you that. When I met him after the war in his office in Hollywood, he showed me books by Hemingway and Faulkner. He said, "I own them." I said, "So do I." So what? Two-fifty a copy. He said, "No, I *own* them."

He had the movie rights.

He did. And Faulkner did a lot of work for him, too. Hawks said, "I would like very much for you to write a script of *The Sun Also Rises*." Never been done. He asked me, "Do you like it?" I said, "Yes and no. I don't like any story where boy meets girl, it's a love story, and you get to the end and find out he has no cock and balls. It's dishonest." I told him I'd write an *honest* script. I gave him an opening scene. A World War I field hospital. The hero's on the operating table. A nurse holds a tin cup and the doctor drops the hero's cock and balls into it. The nurse takes her mask down and it's the leading lady—I forget her name in the book ... Lady Brett. Now at least she knows what's wrong with him. Now it won't be a dishonest progression between them. It'll be something with more heart.... Hawks said, "Are you crazy? At Warner Brothers? You're really crazy."

Hawks never did anything with The Dark Page.

He sold it. At one time he thought of changing one of the characters to a woman for Bogart and Bacall. He did that with *His Girl Friday*. Apparently he couldn't make it work out with my yarn. I don't know why—that's his business. He put up the fifteen thousand dollars. And he sold it for a hundred thousand. Columbia made a picture of it called ... *Scandal* something [*Scandal Sheet*, 1952]. And a friend of mine directed it.

Phil Karlson.

I like him very much. And that book has been published and republished in a lot of places, very classy for me.

You then started selling scripts and stories to the big studios.

I had written three scripts in a row for three different studios—RKO, Warners, MGM. The first one was for Warners. They hated the content. It was called *Murder—How to Get Away with It*. It was an exposé of the police. The second one was for RKO, called *Uncle Sam*. It was an exposé of the immigration act, and involved everyone from the senators on down. It dealt with reactionary people trying to shut the gates on U.S. immigration. I was using real names. It showed how people take advantage of other people who had a couple bucks less. The studio didn't like the way I handled it. They said, "We don't want to do anything like this." They were afraid of the D.A.R. and there were reactionary people in their own script department. And they were just afraid. I used real names, so I said I would change the names. It was no use. They said, "These people are too famous. People will recognize who it is supposed to be."

The third one was for MGM. It was a bank holdup story. L. B. Mayer said, "That's more like it." He read the other two and he liked how I wrote but he didn't like their content. I have a big, big bank robbery. And a guy is investigating the case and you see how he tracks down the men. He sees how the building was hit with grenades, and how the robbers were stationed, and everything is the same way he and his three men took the pillboxes on Omaha Beach. So he knows who the three men are and he tracks them down. He tracks down each man and kills them. In the end he's got a couple of million dollars and he settles down in some island and he lives very happily ever after. And the script ends with some beautiful island girl in his arms and he says, "Who says crime doesn't pay?"

Mayer threw it back. He said American mothers would be outraged for us to say these soldiers could become killers and robbers. So I agreed. They could all be killers as children — the war didn't make them killers, okay! But Mayer thought the mothers would be even more shocked to think their babies were serving with these killer hoods. But most of all, Mayer didn't like that this guy — my hero! — keeps the money and lives happily ever after. He said, "He's got to return the money to the bank and get a medal." I said, "Only an idiot would return the money."

But Mayer still wanted me. They would have put me under contract for very good pay, and it would go up every six months, every year. But I wanted to do my own stuff. When you work on a salary you do what they tell you. I had received excellent money for each script, more than I ever got before. And each one was turned down. They would get excited and then when they read it they got scared. My mother told me, "If you keep writing scripts like this and they pay you like this we'll be very rich. But if they really make one of these damn scripts the bubble is burst!" But I wanted the next time to make sure what I wrote got up on the screen.

I got a call from Robert Lippert, an independent producer. He had heard about my scripts and he wanted to make a picture with me. But he didn't have any money. He told me the price I got for my script, plus twenty-five thousand dollars, was his whole budget for a picture. But this was a chance to get one of my stories done and to direct it.

I could not get him interested in my first idea. I wanted to do a picture about Cassius, the assassin of Caesar. I was fascinated by assassins. This is the man who really kills in cold blood, you understand? But Lippert didn't want it. He didn't want a costume picture like that, men in bedsheets. And I suggested some others, but he didn't want them, too political or whatever. Then I told him the story of Robert Ford, the man who shot Jesse James. And that was the one he wanted. One hundred five thousand dollars for the whole thing, including my script. We did it in ten days.

The real Jesse James was very different from the Tyrone Power Hollywood version, wasn't he?

Jesse James, as a teenager, was a female impersonator. He would dress as a girl and lure soldiers into his cabin like a whore, get them drunk, then his brother Frank would come in, kill them and rob them. That's how Jesse James started his career, as a girl impersonator. He was very beautiful, they say. He became a hero in the folklore, but Jesse James was a despicable character. The first train he robbed was full of wounded soldiers. He killed and robbed the wounded soldiers. Because of what I knew about Jesse James I have been interested and sympathized with Bob Ford. My story was about the emotional degradation of an assassin . . . about a man who killed his friend and what that did to him. Some critics have called it the first "adult" western. There are no horses in my western. No chases, nothing. It could have been a play. Lippert put in a couple of shots—he was afraid—a couple of shots from some western he had made that was just terrible, and he admitted it later because it wasn't that kind of story.

Someone came to you claiming to be the real Jesse James?

There had always been rumors that the real Jesse had not been killed, that it was a fake. And this very old man came to see me, saying he was Jesse James and he could prove it and he wanted some money. Well, I told him that there were a number of police departments that would be very happy to come and pick him up right away. He changed his mind.

As a new director with only ten days to make a movie, you didn't have much time for mistakes.

The first shot I did in my life was the last shot in the picture. An arm comes out of the black and he says to the guy, "Turn around, turn around." Because he shot Jesse James in the back and he doesn't want to shoot a second man in the back. I showed the actor what to do and how to walk and I'm waiting for the guy to do the scene. Nothing happened. The assistant came over and said, "Before they'll start you have to say one word." I said, "What's the word?" He said, "Action." I said, "ACTION!" And they all moved at once . . . Now I was a director. I didn't really know anything about directing, but I think that any writer who describes anything that has any emotional impact has an ability to direct a picture, is very capable of it.

John Ireland and Preston Foster in *I Shot Jesse James* (1949).

Your second film was Baron of Arizona. *Did you get a bigger budget for that one?*

That was an epic—we had fifteen days for that one! It was very successful. And the third one for Lippert was the most successful.

Did Lippert give you a piece of the profits?

No. On the third one, *Steel Helmet,* yes.

What inspired your decision to make Baron of Arizona?

That was a true story, never told before on screen. But what really interested me was the characters, that kind of incestuous situation there, with Price (Vincent Price) and that little girl he raises to be his wife and his meal ticket. This was a very different sort of love story.

Let's talk about your third film, The Steel Helmet. *This was again made on a very low budget and was extremely successful.*

Ten days, one hundred four thousand dollars. It did well, I had a third of it. We had twenty-five extras and I made them act like five hundred—we couldn't afford any more.

It also stirred up a lot of controversy, editorials against you and so forth. Can you discuss this?

This was because I showed an American soldier — a man representing Uncle Sam! — shooting and killing an unarmed prisoner of war, a major in the Chinese Communist party. And I brought out the fact that Germany was not the only country that had concentration camps. We didn't gas people, we didn't burn them or starve them to death, but we had concentration camps. They were called "relocation" camps. In the picture I have a Chinese prisoner say to a Nisei, a Japanese-American, "What the hell are you doing fighting for these white sons-of-bitches? You got the same goddamn slant eyes I have. You know they hate our guts, hate our skin. I even heard that they arrested some of you Japanese-Americans just for being slant-eyed." And this Nisei, this American soldier, says, "You heard about it, it's a fact. My mother and father were arrested. They were separated — one was put in a concentration camp in Arizona, one was put in a concentration camp in California."

Well, the shit hit the fan! Truman or someone in the White House, and the Pentagon, raised hell with it. And this was blown up, this started my relationship with the Pentagon and newspaper columnists. Specifically there was one wonderful guy, an old reporter who had been blinded on a story.

Was that Victor Reisel?

That's it. And he said this picture is anti–American, pro–Communist. This feeds the Reds all the goddamn propaganda they want and I should be investigated by the Pentagon, the army should really find out who the hell I am. And the commie paper, the *Daily Worker,* loved it. . . . "This shows what *beasts* the American soldiers are!" And they called me a reactionary — this *beast* is the lead in my picture, you see? The *hero!* So I'm a reactionary *and* a communist! My mother called me from New York, she said, "Hello, Comrade!" And the Department of Justice and the FBI immediately wanted to know all about me — because it was very touchy in those days, very touchy — are the Communists behind this, are the Reds and the Russians getting their ammo off, all that crap.

Was the relocation of the Japanese-Americans still not well known at that point?

Not too much. But it was fact. If the country did something shameful, it's shameful. It has nothing to do with me. I'm reporting it with a fucking camera.

But I couldn't understand the sensitivity about the scene where the sergeant shoots a prisoner. A big, unwashed American and an emaciated Chinese major — and he shoots him. The Army didn't like what I had done. I said, can I make a call? I got my old company commander on the phone: "Did you ever shoot a prisoner of war?" "Of course!" You can't have law in war. A dogface with an M-1 — that is the law! War is a completely lunatic situation, organized insanity. War is young men killing and getting killed. Sure,

Taking a prisoner in *The Steel Helmet* (1951).

you kill a prisoner of war ... it's all a question of how you feel at that moment—is it raining, are you cold? The idea that you hold your fire in a war situation just because the other guy, who's been trying to kill you, sticks his hands in the air and says, "That's enough, you can take me prisoner now. Geneva Convention..."

You don't think there should be any rules at all in war?

It's not good or bad, it's stupid! You can't have regulations about what happens in combat. Everything goes too fast. A line of action takes maybe two to four minutes. Actually killing and being killed takes that long. You can't take much more. Your eyes tear, you can't shoot. Something happens to your nervous system, very abnormal to it, from your head to your fingers. It's worse than when you're driving like hell and suddenly you have to stomp on the brake. Another thing that's never used in a war picture, is a lot of young men just died of heart attack, they just dropped. You can have a heart examination and you're perfectly fine and five minutes later you drop dead.

What was the significance of the giant Buddha's still standing after everything around it has been destroyed?

I used it visually. Do you remember, I put the plasma in the Buddha's palm. Letting the Buddha stand after all that destruction, this happens with these religious relics and no one can explain it. There's a huge Buddha in Japan, Kamakura, and it was all that remained standing after a major earthquake. Strange, huh?

The third one was an extremely successful picture, and I was asked to go to every studio. Mayer, Warner, Spitz and Goetz at Universal, Cohn at Columbia. They all told me about the enormous amount of money I could make. They were ready to give me deals left and right. It wasn't that they had seen my picture and thought I had made a great picture. It was the time I took to shoot the picture and the money it took in that appealed. If I had made a picture in ten days and it didn't bring in a dollar of course they wouldn't have been interested. It had nothing to do with your individual talent. I met them all. The last man I met was Zanuck. And he had run my other two pictures and *Steel Helmet* many times. He said, "What story do you want to make first?"

He talked story rather than business — was that what made Zanuck's offer more appealing than the others?
    Yes! That was it — he said what story, anything you want to shoot. I said, "Something that hasn't been done." He said, "Everything's been done and I did it." I disagreed. So we bet a thousand cigars. He said, "I'll win." I said, "I'll win. But if I win I don't want your cigars." Because he smoked denicotinized cigars. Just like coffee without caffeine. And I wouldn't get a kick out of smoking one of his cigars. So I said, "I'll give you the title in two words and you will know you've lost a thousand cigars." I said, "It's called *Red Square*. I will do twenty-four hours in the life of a city in the Soviet Union. I will show what every aspect of life is there. No one knows. What is a toilet like there? How does a couple get engaged, get married? If there's a murder how is a murder solved? How do you get a job? What is a department store like? We would find out everything through the eyes of a young man, a soldier. That's the story."
    He said no. First of all, he didn't want anything to do with that country. He said no and that was it. But from there I made a deal with him and did seven pictures. Six months a year I belonged to 20th Century–Fox, six months a year I could do anything I wanted. Perfect.

You were a great admirer of Zanuck, weren't you?
    I was crazy about him.

I've gotten the impression he was more respectful of writers than of his other employees.
    He went for anyone *behind* the camera. He didn't like actors — unfortunately for the actors.

Zanuck did what all studio people should do. He got excited. If he liked your project he was very encouraging. And you get more excited and you want to go make the picture for him and show him how good you are — "if you think that was good, I'm really going to show you!" And when Zanuck said "Okay," you made the picture. *One man!* This is different from today. Today you go to the average big production company and they have fifty executives and fifty meetings and everybody has to say "okay." You understand? That's different from telling one man your story and if he likes it that means you make it. When you leave his office you start to make a picture. Today it can take years.

But Zanuck would get very excited. And he would get up in his office — a big office with elk heads and moose heads all over the goddamn place — and he'd act a scene for you, a guy carrying a body, very visual — don't forget he wrote all those Rin-Tin-Tin stories when he started. So you can see how excited he would get with a story.

Your first film for Fox was Fixed Bayonets, *another Korean War story. I suppose the studio was hoping lightning would strike twice with you and the war.*

He said, "Listen. Your picture is a hit and the most controversial thing to hit the country. You're a Red and you're a reactionary. Everybody's going to copy it, it's the first Korean War picture. We want to do the same thing." I said, "I just did it." He said, "It won't be the same. The others will copy the last one, this one won't." So I did *Fixed Bayonets.* And that was the story of a man, a soldier, who *cannot* kill. And by the end he has made himself able to kill, and then he is *accepted.*

It's a variation on the sane/insane paradox in Big Red One — *what is normal, admirable behavior, not wanting to kill anybody, becomes abnormal in war.*

That's my story. That's what war is about, killing and death and staying alive. I don't like war movies that are about the girl back home or politics or stealing gold or whatever the hell bullshit...

When your characters are dying I don't think you ever hear any noble speeches or confessions.

It very seldom happens that way. What you hear is screaming: "JESUS! OH SHIT!"

The battle on the ice in Fixed Bayonets *is very memorable.*

I did that in a way that you get real reactions there. I had the set cleared and we iced it, and when the actors came back they were falling on their asses, with explosions going off and everything. That was real panic you see.

Was anyone injured?

Gene Evans inspects another casualty in *Fixed Bayonets* (1951).

This was the first war movie that had real casualties. The stuntmen would get a sprain or hurt an arm and they'd be off the picture normally. I found out they didn't get paid when they got hurt. So I kept them on the payroll and used them to play casualties. So all the casualties you see in that picture are real casualties!

After making a film for a major studio, what advantages did that have over your independent productions?

You get to have more people, the best in the business. There are technical things you can do with that kind of staff—tear down a wall, crane shots, whatever it is. But it doesn't matter to me. With a studio there is a little more supervision, more people watching you to see you aren't throwing their money away. As an independent you don't get as much of that. But whenever somebody puts up the money there's going to be some of that.

Did you try to get Park Row *made at Fox before you did it independently?*

Zanuck didn't want to do it my way. He hated my title, he wanted to call it *In Old New York*. He had a big hit called *In Old Chicago*. He wanted me to make it a musical, in color, with Dan Dailey as the guy who jumped off the Brooklyn Bridge, and Mitzi Gaynor as the first barmaid in New York.

So I made that picture with my own money. One hundred percent. And

Gene Evans, crusading newspaper editor, *Park Row* (1952).

most of the money went for that set, that street. I wanted it to be exactly the way it was in 1886. I had a set built four stories high. You would never see all of that set. The designers thought I was crazy. You never build four stories for a set, crazy. But I had to see it all. I had to know that everything was there, exact in every detail. And it was very authentic, that set. Some of those buildings still remain down there. The street was the picture. My cast was not well known—Gene Evans was in *Helmet*, and Mary Welch—it was her only picture, she died young.

I lost all my money on that picture. Never made a cent. But it was a great thrill for me because I had a lot of memories on that street.

The best audience I had for that picture was when it was run for the Newspaper Publishers and Editors Association. They met at the Waldorf once a year. Representatives of over seventeen hundred daily newspapers. And they loved this picture, they applauded, they cried. And the son of one of my characters in the picture—Mergenthaler—came up to me and thanked me.

See, there were things in there, facts, details, that other newspapermen could respond to. Something very personal. And a few years ago, in Strausbourg, I was a jury president for the first festival for both cinema and press. There were a lot of men there from Woodward and Bernstein on down. And I met a man in the lobby, an important magazine editor, and he came up to me and told me he was never so moved in his life as when he saw *Park Row*. The emotional problems the newsman in the picture had, the things he was fighting and the things they misunderstood about him. And he knew every scene in the picture, and it all meant something to him. And that came from nowhere because that picture was made in '52. I was moved, the way that hit him. And I thought, I want to hit all men like I hit him.

What's the genesis of Pickup on South Street? *Dwight Taylor gets the story credit.*

This writer, Dwight Taylor, the son of Laurette Taylor, asked me if I wouldn't get the studio to buy his story, an original script of his. It was a courtroom drama. I don't like them—Billy Wilder made it work but that's about it. I followed courtroom cases as a reporter. They take seven months to play out. I don't like them. His story was about a criminal and a female attorney who falls in love with him. The studio bought it but I said to Zanuck, "Instead, let's do a different kind of criminal story. Let's do a crime story about a cannon—a pickpocket." I wanted to do a story set among the real criminal class. I like them. When my wife and I got to Paris, our first day on the subway, she got her purse picked, by the second stop. She said, "How did he do it?" I said, "Whaddaya mean—it's an art!" So this was my hero—a cannon. And I wrote the girl character—she's not sexy enough to be a hooker, not smart enough to be a housewife. And we had the big spy case with Fuchs, and I wrote that into it. And Zanuck said, "What kind of characters have you got here? You've gotta have a 'nice' boy and girl subplot in this thing." But I didn't change it.

Richard Widmark is a perfect anti-hero in this. He makes you root for him but until the very end he doesn't do a thing to deserve it.

That's the reason I wanted Widmark. He was *perfect*. He could be a heavy, he could be the lead. He could go either way.

Was the whole film done in the studio?

In the studio and in some not-so-beautiful parts of Los Angeles.

It's got the most authentic looking New York sets—everything looks coated in grime.

Yeah. Did you like my subway set?

Yes. The fight scene at the end is very brutal for that era in Hollywood. I wanted to ask you, was that instinctive, to shoot it that way, or did you decide in advance, "I'm going to make this the most brutal fight scene I can stage"?

It was planned. I knew how I wanted that to look and feel. I had those stairs there so I could have Widmark dragging the agent, Kiley's face over each step. I wanted to have them hear his chin smack every step.

Jean Peters with Vic Perry as "Lightnin' Louie" in _Pickup on South Street_ (1953).

Tell me about "Lightnin' Louie" — he's like a fully developed character that you see once for a couple of minutes and never again. I understand the guy who played him was a magician?

Yeah, a magician, sleight-of-hand, named Vic Perry. He looked the part, because I wanted this character to be someone who loved food and never stopped eating even when he was selling information. And he was a card sharp so he was very good with his hands and could do the bit with the chopsticks, picking up the money, perfect. He never even looks up. This was the only part this man ever acted, too.

Pickup — and you — have been lumped in with the anticommunist fervor of the '50s, but no one in the film — except for the FBI agent, who comes off unlikable and self-righteous — seems to know or care anything about politics or government.

From this picture I had my second run-in with the FBI, and J. Edgar Hoover. He was very disturbed by this picture. He had had some things to say about _The Steel Helmet,_ and now he was disturbed about _Pickup._ We had a meeting at Romanoff's, a restaurant in Hollywood. Well, first of all he said that he didn't like many things in it. He did not like that the hero — who's really a heavy, a pickpocket — is told by the FBI that they want him to cooperate so we can get this communist agent. And the FBI says, "Doesn't the United

States mean anything to you?" Hoover hated that. What kind of thing is that for an American to say? This was the time of flag-waving, '51, '52. I said, "That's his *character!*" It's not me. If it were another character he might say, "By God, I'll do anything for my country!" That doesn't prove I'm a rah-rah guy, that's *his* character. This is the trouble with a lot of critics, too. They're biased, they see with one eye, hear with one ear. You have these cinéastes who are politically inclined, and if the picture is going the way they think, it's a good picture, if it's going against, it's a bad picture. They look at it from their political viewpoint. They aren't seeing it from a writer's viewpoint. You know what I'm talking about. A writer has to write every viewpoint. I can have a character say one thing or another thing—it doesn't make me anti–American, or this or that.

I have another character in there, an informer, played magnificently by Thelma Ritter. And the agent says to her, "What the hell have you got against selling information to a commie?" And she says, "I don't know anything about commies. All I know is I don't like 'em." And that was the way a lot of people felt. This was a boogeyman, and she expressed what a lot of people felt.

But to get back to the great J. Edgar, he found many things wrong with the picture. He hated the idea that I had a character played by Widmark who was willing to deal with both Russia and the United States government. All he cared about was the money—self interest. And Hoover said, "How could an American think of money at a time like that?" And then he objected—he was shocked—at the way I had one of his agents working with a New York City cop, bribing a stool pigeon to get information. Hoover said, "No, the Department of Justice would not do that!" But I had been in the precincts. And I saw cops talking and haggling with FBI guys about the price they would give to a fink. I saw them take money out and put it in the cop's kitty. The Sixteenth Precinct in New York City.

Some would say Hoover's success with the FBI was largely due to his handling of the press and public relations.

He had been in charge of a group of attorneys that became very, very famous through a Warner Bros. film called *G-Men,* and people from Jimmy Cagney to Jimmy Stewart eulogizing him. And that's perfectly all right. The thing that I didn't know and has been exposed in the last few years, I guess, is that he was a very devious head of an organization that blackmailed to keep his personal position of power, and at the same time pulling this entire organization up with him. He kept enough information to make things go his way in the White House. That's true and that's a good story. That's a story I'd like to make about J. Edgar. I wouldn't make him a heavy, I wouldn't make him a hero. I could do the same thing with the Iron Duke, for Christ's sake. He whipped the hell out of Napoleon, he was the hero of Britain on Monday, and the same week they began to stone his carriage. Lauded and then loathed.

With all his power, though, he didn't exert enough pressure to get the offending scenes in Pickup *cut or changed.*

That was Zanuck. Zanuck told him, "Mr. Hoover, you don't know movies!" Zanuck didn't care about politics, he cared about a good story. The story had nothing to do with politics. This was a hero who didn't care about Uncle Joe *or* Uncle Sam.

In fact, the French released a dubbed version with the spy plot changed to drug smuggling.

The president of Fox, Spyros Skouros called me in London. He told me, "France says *Pickup*'s an anticommunist plot. They don't want to run it like that." I said, "Let them fool with it...." And they changed it. And it was redone in South Africa years later, *Pickup in Capetown,* and he works on a bus.

Zanuck offered *Pickup* to the Venice Film Festival. Each studio offered one film for the festival to choose from. They took *Pickup.* And it won the Bronze Lion—from commie judges! Zanuck laughed like hell.

Hell and High Water *seems one of your least personal films. Would you go along with that?*

I don't particularly like the picture but I made it for one reason and I'll make it brief. They had already made a few Cinemascope pictures and unfortunately what they had expected didn't happen. They wanted signed contracts with theaters all over the world. This would mean reconstruction for the screens and the new projectors. They wanted it in writing. But the theater owners resisted Cinemascope. They complained about these first releases, "Well, these are kind of stagey. Everything stays in one place." They didn't see any movement on screen, the camera never moved for three minutes. The screen was so wide that characters could keep walking and the camera wouldn't have to move to keep them on screen. There was not enough "action" on screen for the audiences.

Now I don't really pay attention to the technical side of the camera. I assume that the cameraman and his operators are experts in their field. I show exactly what I want and the movement, but technically they have to worry about how to do it. And I've had a lot of luck with that. The studio came to me and said this is very important, we've got a lot of money in this, and we want you to direct this picture. Work on the goddamned script, whatever you want, but make the picture. And just forget that it's Cinemascope, that's the important thing.

And that's what I did. I moved the camera, I panned it, I went up and down, I did dolly shots with it *inside* the submarine. I have some fighting at the end with all the different weapons, light, medium, heavy, and I staged that like a ballet, with the camera swinging around. And this is what they

A brawl in the close quarters of a submarine, from *Hell and High Water* (1954).

wanted, to get the Cinemascope camera away from that stagey look, and it worked for them. They were very, very happy, and they had three world premieres, in L.A., New York and London, so the theater owners would go to a premiere in the different areas. They had George Jessel emceeing one, and Noel Coward in London, and I forget who they had in the other one. But it was important for the studio and it was a success for them.

To me this was a kind of old-fashioned fun adventure story, nothing more. But ironically enough, when I did a walk-on for Steven Spielberg in *1941*, he showed me his car and in his trunk was a print that he carries with him all the time—he loved it and it was *Hell and High Water*.

Zanuck put his mistress Bella Darvi in the picture. Did you have any problems getting a performance from her?

No, wonderful girl. The only thing I can add is that when I was working on the script, I made the female character a highly educated physicist who was the daughter of a Nobel Prize–winning physicist. And Zanuck said, "Look, I'd like you to use her in the picture, but this is a very strong part, a starring role." I said, "Yes, it's a leading role. She has to fight, love, kill, command." I couldn't make just a girl there, with no reason for a girl there. But there would be a reason for a physicist to have an assistant, and I didn't mind the assistant being his daughter, and carrying out all the elements I wanted. Zanuck said "great," and it worked out very nicely.

House of Bamboo was your first film shot on location, in Japan. What sort of problems did this present?

This was great. We went everywhere. It was the first American picture shot in Japan—no one had seen these scenes on a screen before.

The colors are very striking in the street scenes—bright red objects even in long shots—was this just the way things were on the streets or were these things on screen by design?

By design. For the most part, by design. When you've got color you use it. Sometimes you use it for a mood. You can play with it. In that picture I start out with very little color. With the train, Mt. Fuji in the back—everything is white except for that train, that dark train where death occurs. And only when the titles come on, and the woman goes to the police, do the colors start to hit you.

This is another one of your ambiguous heroes. On the one hand he's a good guy, opposing the gangsters. But to do so he has to be a spy and betray the people who befriend him—and the Robert Ryan character even saves his life.

That's right, that's the heart of the story. Ryan saves him and he doesn't know why. He says, "Does anybody know why I saved his goddamned life?" Because it's against the rule of this gang—you shoot your wounded so they don't talk to the police. See, he's getting closer to Stack, he feels something for him that makes him drop his defenses. And Stack, this cop, he uses that to destroy Ryan. Ryan is a criminal, but he's honest with his *emotions*. Stack is a cop, he obeys the law, but he's *dishonest* with what he speaks, with his feelings.

The gang plans their crimes like a military operation. This sounds like that earlier script about the D-Day veterans who rob the bank. Was part of House of Bamboo *adapted from that screenplay?*

You caught that, huh? No, it wasn't the script. But I took some of that situation, the idea.

Did you do research for Run of the Arrow? *It's a very different view of the Indians than in most Hollywood westerns.*

I did a helluva lot of research for that. I got material from Washington about each of the tribes. I didn't want to do the usual movie where the Indians are like a joke. A lot of what has been shown in movies with American Indians, the massacres, the packs of killers, this was a tiny portion of a tribe here and there—like we have teenagers in gangs, killing people. But I thought I would do a film where the Indians, if they didn't win, they were not destroyed at the end of the picture. And this film was shown by the Indian Commission in Washington and some of the tribes wrote to me with invitations.

I don't know if it's Rod Steiger's personality or the character you wrote, but I don't find him very likable.

He's a bad loser, nobody likes a bad loser. He's filled with hate, he's lost the war. But this is how a lot of people feel.

You contrast him with General Lee at the beginning, who accepts his defeat with nobility.

Yes. And Steiger can't accept that yet.

I read that you shot "The Run" the way you did because Rod Steiger hurt his foot and couldn't do it.

That's right, he was out. So I kept the camera on the feet. I would have done something close to that, anyway, but it worked, and a lot of people commented on it. And we also used some beautiful long shots there, too. I had a very good cameraman for that and we got some shots where you see these small figures moving across the landscape, like two dots.

What did you mean by the tag at the end—"only you can write the end to this story"?

Just what it says. That story is still not over. These problems, these hates, are still alive, still not settled.

By the way, ironically enough, I was making *Run of the Arrow* at RKO and Gene Fowler came in. And he was one of my editors on a paper years before—my father was gone, died, and he was like a poppa for me. And he gave me the incentive right from the start. He said, "One day you'll use these

Angie Dickinson and Gene Barry on patrol behind enemy lines in *China Gate* (1957).

things, situations, characters, somewhere along the line—they're *great*." And Gene came in with his son, Gene Jr., and he was an editor for Fritz Lang, and he cut my picture. So his father was my editor and the son was my editor. I thought it was a funny situation.

*You made a film about Vietnam in 1957—*China Gate*—long before most Americans had heard of the place.*

Not Vietnam, Indochina. Very important. This was a French colony then. And here's what I didn't like about the colonial powers—French, British, Dutch, whoever—that they put up an umbrella that they were doing good in these other countries, that they were "helping the people." Instead of saying there was a lot of *money* on the goddamn soil, and we want it. And I wrote a prologue about this. I received a call from the French Consul in Los Angeles. He had read the script and saw a rough cut of the picture. And this was a man named Romain Gray.

Who wrote the original story of White Dog?

Yes. And this is how I met him. And he said, "I work for France. Can you do something about that introduction?" Not whether it was accurate. I said, "If this was about Italy, what would you say?" He said, "I'd say the hell with it." I fell in love with him.

But this was the first movie that ever said the words "Ho Chi Minh." It didn't mean a thing to anybody at that time. I had a big goddamn blowup of him. And Zanuck came on the set and said, "Who the hell is that?" I said, "Ho Chi Minh." He said, "Oh yeah, I remember the name from the script. What was it about him I liked?" I said, "He was the assistant pastry cook at a London hotel who wound up the head of a nation." Zanuck said, "You hear that? That's the kind of guy I like! A pastry cook, goddamn it!" The whole Horatio Alger thing appealed to him. He didn't care a damn about the political color in this case because it was the French involved.

But this wasn't about politics—it could have been set anywhere. This was an anti-racist story. A white man has a child with a half-caste Asian and he deserts them. The kid looks Oriental and he can't take it. And when they meet again, she says, "What do you want, a piece of paper in advance guaranteeing the angle of the baby's eyes? And Nat Cole, another soldier, says, "You sonofabitch, you don't want this kid, I'll take care of him. I always wanted a kid. I don't care what he looks like!"

Nat played that part, but I never used the word "black" in that script. My agent then was Nat Goldstein, and I named the character "Goldy." And I told him I want this guy to play Goldy. He said, "But it doesn't say a *black* in the script." See, usually in a script it would say what it was in the script, for the casting department—black, yellow, skinny, short, ugly. But this was just a *person*. And Nat read the script and he liked that it wasn't a "black" part. You know how much he got when he did that picture? Five thousand bucks. You know what he got just for singing "Three Coins in the Fountain" behind the credits of that picture? Seventy-five thousand dollars.

Is it true that Marilyn Monroe was originally supposed to star in Forty Guns?

Marilyn Monroe wanted to do the picture. A woman riding with an army of forty men—that appealed to her. She wasn't really right for the part, but it might have been something. Stanwyck did the part and she really had what I wanted for that relationship between the brother and sister. Stanwyck gave you a lot, whatever you needed she was ready. The shot where she is being dragged by the horse, that's her, not a stuntman. And we had some problems with it, technical things, and she agreed to do it several times until we got it right.

A real trouper.

Yeah, she was black-and-blue after that.

They made you change your original ending for Forty Guns, *didn't they?*

Yes. My ending as I wrote it was stronger, it went all the way. When

Sullivan makes up his mind he has to kill Stanwyck's brother, that's all he knows. He turns killer. What he thinks of Stanwyck doesn't matter to him now. And the brother holds Stanwyck in front of him as a shield, so Sullivan shoots them both. And I had them both killed, Stanwyck and the brother. And Sullivan just keeps walking, doesn't stop.

There was something you saw in a lot of pictures. *High Noon* and so on, and I didn't like it. The heavy grabs the leading lady and makes the hero drop his gun or he'll shoot her. And usually the girl pulls away so the good guy can kill the bad guy. And this is stupid—if she can get away that easy there is no point in having him grab her. So I wanted to do this scene in a way the audience isn't expecting, where the hero shoots even when the heavy is still hiding behind the girl.

I had to change it because the studio wouldn't let it go with Stanwyck getting killed like that. She had to live and they had to go off together into the sunset.

It's still a pretty strong climax. There aren't many westerns where the hero shoots an unarmed woman.

Yeah, it works. I would have liked my original ending more—it would have had even more impact. And I preferred my original title for the thing. You still hear it in a song in the picture. I wanted to call it *Woman with a Whip.*

In The Crimson Kimono *you approach the subject of racism again from an unusual angle.*

That picture I made for one reason. I wanted to show how racism can come from anywhere. In this case two cops, one Japanese, one white, fall in love with a white girl. And the girl picks the Japanese cop. Now the white cop hates his partner. And the Japanese thinks it's racial hatred: "You hate me because the girl preferred a Japanese to you, a white man." But the white cop says, "You're wrong. It's not race, it's personal. I'm mad because you stole my girl."

The opening, where the stripper gets killed on the street, is very striking. How did you shoot that?

For that I wanted a big girl, over six feet tall, running nude through the street, and I had the cameras hidden so I could get the real reaction of people seeing an almost naked girl running down Sixth and Main Street. And most of the people she passed didn't even turn around.

I wanted her to fall right in the main cross-section there, right in the middle of all the traffic passing. This was real traffic, except that I had father and daughter stunt drivers who would know this naked girl would run in front and be shot. It's real traffic, but it's timed, they're in the lead. So we did it, hidden cameras, and I shot my gun into the sky and she falls. And as soon as

John Ericson uses sister Barbara Stanwyck as a shield—to no avail—in *Forty Guns* (1957).

we got it we bundled her into the car and took off. And then the shit hit the fan. A lot of people heard the shot, saw the girl fall, and they called the cops. And the cops come and they're looking for the body of this big stripper. I still had to get a close shot and we couldn't go back there for hours, until the cops cleared off.

Originally I wanted to start the picture with a camera in a chopper. I wanted to start about fifteen hundred feet in the air, above city hall, and we come down, down, and come right in front of the theater and come right up to a poster of the stripper and dissolve inside to the live girl on stage in the same position. But there was some law in L.A. that you can't fly low over a city unless it's an emergency—it's too dangerous with those choppers. I even became involved with getting Columbia to try and bribe the pilot to do it anyway. That didn't work out. He figured out how much we would pay him and how much he would lose if they took his license away for five years and he said it wasn't worth it.

Underworld U.S.A. *is a kind of variation on the situation in* Pickup—Robertson *is helping the police get the gangsters but it's strictly self-serving on his part. He's out for revenge.*

That's realistic. That character wouldn't help the police because it's the goody-goody thing to do. He does it for personal reasons—like ninety-nine point nine percent of people do things.

Interracial romance blooms between Victoria Shaw and cop James Shigeta in *Crimson Kimono* (1959).

This was a Dumas story. I didn't hide it. One of the characters is reading *Count of Monte Cristo*. This picture was a request on the part of the studio. The title belonged to a magazine serial by a newspaperman, bought by Bogart. A producer bought it after Bogart died and there was a lot of money invested so they had to do something. But the magazine story was a period piece about the prohibition era and they didn't want to do that. So I wrote something original.

It's one of the first gangster movies to equate the mob with a big, efficient corporation.

I did research. I got information from the Department of Justice in Washington showing the estimated profits that were made from organized criminal activities — prostitution, gambling, drugs, labor unions. And if you realized how successful they were in their businesses you wouldn't want to go into any other line of work, you see what I'm saying? But they made me take a lot of that out — the censors were afraid everyone would go out and try to join the rackets.

They cut another scene you said was one of the best you ever shot — the strike of the whores.

Fuller (in sunglasses) shooting scenes for *The Crimson Kimono* on the streets of "Little Tokyo."

Yes. The whores go on strike. And we see a map of the United States and the legs of hookers—closing their legs all across the map. They wouldn't let me keep it.

Shock Corridor *combines a lot of your themes in one story. The insane asylum is a good metaphor for the outside world—is that what drew you to the setting?*
I had been interested in the subject of mental hospitals for a long time.

"I die inside when you kiss me": Cliff Robertson and Dolores Dorn, *Underworld U.S.A.*'s unlucky lovers.

When I was a reporter I was taken into a ward for the insane by a cop and he tried to pull a joke on me and lock me in there. And I considered doing a story in this setting for some time, an exposé. The insane are very interesting—because they are a lot like you and me. Most people are a lot closer to this than they want to believe. So I came up with a story, with the reporter. There was a reporter, a famous female reporter who made a big exposé of the insane asylum on Wards Island by pretending to be insane. So I had this.

And then there was the timing. At that time in the United States there were many things happening, big changes, people tearing each other apart, and I thought I could represent some things about the country, how it was like an insane asylum. You had the black and white thing. You had the war veterans who deserted. You have the man like an Oppenheimer, with the A-bomb. I have the black man, kind of a James Meredith student in a white Southern school—and he cracks, he can't take being this symbol to both sides. And he goes around to the other side in his mind, thinks he's in the Klan, hates blacks, recites all the words of the white bigots. And I have the nuclear scientist, a brilliant mind, can't cope with what he's created, the nuclear bomb, and his mind becomes like a two-year-old.

You made this and Naked Kiss *with a legendary cinematographer, Stanley Cortez. Did you two work well together?*

We worked beautifully. He did *Magnificent Ambersons* with Welles and some sensational work on *Night of the Hunter*, directed by Charles Laughton. He maybe would have liked to do something a little more surrealistic with *Shock Corridor*—and I would have, too, but we didn't have the budget.

The scene where Breck imagines the rain and lightning in the corridor is pretty surreal.

That was the last thing we shot. That set was not really designed to be flooded with water like that—there was no place for the water to drain off. They would have thrown us out on our asses if they knew what we were doing to that set. I shot with two cameras so we could get it over with and get the hell out.

Were budget considerations the reason you used the home movie footage for the fantasy scenes?

It was 16mm widescreen, unsqueezed. I wanted it to have an unusual feel, very different from the black-and-white of the rest. This was stuff I shot with my own camera, some of it from Japan while making *Bamboo* and some of it from the time I spent with a tribe in Brazil.

Was the Brazil trip connected to a film project?

Yes. I had a story set in the Matto Grosso, among the Jivaro. It was about a tiger hunter and there's a story with a husband and wife. I stayed with the Indians there for six weeks. I was their guest. These were head-shrinkers and they shrunk a head for me and I filmed it. Wayne and Tyrone Power would have done the picture, but the studio couldn't get insurance to take the stars into the jungle. They couldn't leave Rio. They thought it was too dangerous.

What was your impulse in making The Naked Kiss?

What interested me was the type of mentality found in many small towns in the United States. And the people they look up to and the people they look down at. And I have one of those local heroes who's the son of the mayor or the bank president and he's rich and a war hero, and they don't know that the sonofabitch is a child molester. The man they all look up to is the lowest of the low. And the one they despise, the hooker, is above him. They're hypocrites. And I have a speech in there at the end where she tells them what they are, she rubs it in so they know it. And the theater owners wanted this speech out. They said, "You don't need that speech." I said, "I think I do." They said, "We're not going to be able to go all out for this picture with that speech in there. People aren't going to want to hear this speech, because it's about *them*."

The business about the "Naked Kiss" itself, did you make that concept up, or is that real hooker parlance, about the pervert's kiss?
    No. That's parlance.

The film has one of the most startling openings I've ever seen.
    Did that hit you? With that opening you know this is going to be different. You don't know what's going to happen but it's going to be different. This could have been one of those stories they've done a million times, the girl from the wrong side of the tracks makes good with the nice rich guy.

When the leading lady is introduced as a violent, bald prostitute, the audience can never be sure how this character will end up.
    Yeah.

Did you use hand-held cameras for the subjective shots?
    The camera was strapped to the actors, to their chests. And the girl hits the camera lens. And then it's strapped to her and she's beating the pimp. And then she's staring straight into the camera again, putting on her lipstick, the camera's the mirror. It's very direct, like a shot in the face, the whole thing. I open with a straight cut, no dissolve, no fade-in. I want to grab you.

Did you have any trouble with the censors of the time?
    No. There were a few questions asked. They would have been interested in the way I would deal with the child being molested. But there was nothing censorable there. It was all faces, reactions. You don't see anything, but you know what has gone on. But some people were shocked by this story, they want to close their eyes to these things.

When did you become aware of the critical reaction to your work among the French film critics?

I was not really aware of the cinema in France, with the exceptions of some films that had great success in America—the films of Duvivier and Pagnol. An actor named Victor Francen who was in *Hell and High Water* showed me an article in *Cahiers du Cinéma*. It was an article by Luc Moullet. Victor translated the entire article for me. And it called me a cinematic Marlowe, Christopher Marlowe—I thought, this writer's gotta be drunk!

Then in the sixties I had an idea I would move to the French Riviera and write down *The Big Red One*. I went there in '65. Two French producers came to see me. They had money, they said, and wanted to talk about producing a film. I told them an idea I had, to do a poem on screen. *Flowers of Evil* by Baudelaire. The poem would be the screenplay. Every line was a shot. This had everything. We didn't make it.

I got a call from Godard. He wanted to talk to me. He was doing a picture, *Pierrot le Fou,* and he wanted me to appear in it. I asked him what the scene was about. It was a party scene and I'm supposed to talk to Belmondo. I said, "Good. Standing next to Belmondo I'll look like Alain Delon."

These directors like Godard had a different way of making a film. It wasn't like an American movie where you know where you're going from start to finish. In an American movie you can make changes, little touches, but you know as you start the picture that the son is going to kill the mother, and not vice versa. But with Godard it was different. Anything could happen—the son might not feel like killing the mother or she might kill the son . . . or marry him!

Did you write your lines out or was it really improvised?

I didn't write it. I said it. I made it up there. Godard says, "Belmondo will ask you a question: what is cinema? And you answer what you want." I made my answer short. I'm not going to make it long, I'll end up on the cutting room floor. Now I'm talking as an actor, an *actor!* I'm certainly not going to say anything to cut myself out of the picture. So I made it as brief as possible. And Godard liked it very much. He was very happy. He kissed me. He said, "It was perfect. It fits the movie perfectly." I said, "You son-of-a-bitch, that fits all movies."

Later, I saw some of his pictures and I realized he had taken things from my pictures and used them in his own. I said to him, "You're a goddamned thief! A plagiarist!" Godard said, "In America, plagiarism, in France . . . *hommage!*"

What about some of these bigger acting parts you did later—how did they work out? The ones for Wim Wenders . . .

I did a few bits with him. In *American Friend* I'm supposed to be a Mafia producer of pornographic films. I take a train ride from Hamburg and then later I get murdered. With *Hammett,* he asked me please do one line. And he surprised me, he had my cameraman Joe Biroc, and most of the extras were people I used as extras — they were all there waiting for me in the pool room. And he asked me if I knew anything about Hammett. I said no. I knew he was a writer and he was Lillian Hellman's lover. And he was a Pinkerton man for a while and then turned the other way politically against that. And I think he's wonderful. I like that mythical private eye, 'cause I've known private eyes and they're nothing like that. They're fat asses, sitting in their cars with sandwiches and coffee, following someone's wife around for hours. Or they try and pick up a car you haven't kept up the payments on. And that's what private detectives are. No gun, very seldom anything involving the police.

So Wim said, "Hammett will come down, and you're in the pool room" — with Brian Keith, from *Run of the Arrow* — "and he'll say hello and you say hello. And then you can say something about some fighters you liked when you were a kid." So I said, "I don't know anything about him. Tell me a little more. Is that his real name, Dashiell Hammett?" He said, "No, his real name is Samuel Dashiell Haammett." So I call him Sam in the scene. He asks how's the new baby. I say, "Great. We named it after you — Samantha." They shot the whole movie over and cut out everybody but the star, but my scene is still in it.

Then *The State of Things*. I play a cameraman named Joe, after Joe Biroc. We went to Portugal for that. And I have a scene in there, we're going to Lisbon to catch a plane and he said, "I'll put a camera with you and ask questions and you answer." And he asked, "Do you prefer shooting in black-and-white or color?" I said, "That's a silly question. The world is color. There's no reason for black-and-white. I don't like gray grass." A lot of people say, "Oh, black-and-white is great for some things — streets at night, dark alleys and all that." But in fact there are many colors at night in dingy neighborhoods, all-night coffee pots with lousy neon lights, red and blue — you'd never see that in black-and-white. So that was it with Wim Wenders, I did three.

Then I did something for Steven Spielberg, for *1941*. He wanted me to play Stilwell. I said no. That's bad casting, it's ridiculous for me to be Stilwell. Then he wanted me to say, "Big Red One." I said I couldn't do that. He said, "If you won't say 'Big Red One' will you say 'Red One Alert'?" I said I didn't want to say that. So I said something else, and that was it.

I did a picture for Dennis Hopper, who was the lead in Wim's picture, *American Friend*.

That was The Last Movie. *Did you have a clear idea what Hopper was doing there?*

Dennis had done a very successful movie, *Easy Rider*, that had knocked Hollywood on its ass. And they gave him his head on his next one, and he got his gun off on that whatever the hell way he wanted. We went to Peru. I played a director, making a cowboy movie. The picture was not commercial,

The D-Day invasion, from *The Big Red One* (1980).

and the studio did not know what to do with it. Dennis was not able to do anything for years after that.

And Coppola called me for an acting part one time. He tested me for the part of Meyer Lansky in *Godfather II*. Lee Strasberg did the part. Coppola didn't think I looked old enough, sick enough. But later he said to me, "When you see *Apocalypse Now* you'll see some flags on a post and you'll see the Big Red One." And he put that in for me. I think Coppola is a wonderful guy, in addition to being a helluva talent.

Who are some of the other directors you admire?

Many, many . . . Ford, Hawks, Fritz Lang. And I got to know many of these men, and they were wonderful characters, *great* . . . Wellman and Raoul Walsh. And Joe Mankiewicz and Billy Wilder, men of wit and great, great humor.

I read some glowing remarks that John Ford made about you. Were you two close?

We were very good friends. We visited each other's sets. He had a rough sense of humor. He would call my home every year on June 6—anniversary of D-Day. And instead of saying, "Happy anniversary," or something, he would say, "Fuck the Big Red One" and hang up. My wife would pick up the phone and she didn't understand he was just kidding. He was a Navy man.

Can you describe your concept for The Big Red One?

I don't like propaganda films. I never made a propaganda or a hurrah picture about war. I did a picture called *Merrill's Marauders* for Warner Bros. And I don't know if you remember it, but the end of that picture was based on fact and I had hit it hard, gave it a helluva impact—where General Merrill tells the small group of survivors they have to go on fighting. And he dies and they fight and they're killed. I shot the scene, the final battle. And Warners left that out. Now when he drops dead they say, "Let's go," and they dissolve to a stock shot of Fifth Avenue and soldiers marching. And you hear a voice talking about the glory of the United States and the men who fought the wonderful battles. And this was not my ending—my ending does not try to induce you to join the Army. There was a review in *Newsweek,* and the critic raved about the picture, said it had the effect of a newsreel even though it was with actors. And then it said *but* the only Hollywood touch in the whole picture was that stock footage at the end—that Warners had cut into the movie.

I ran *The Big Red One* at the Pentagon. Seven hundred officers were there to see it, including General George Patton III. I met him at 20th Century-Fox when he was a captain. Now he's a three star, bigger and wider than his father. And he loved the picture. "But," he said, "with this picture we'll never get anybody to volunteer for the army." He said, "It has NO RECRUITMENT FLAVOR." And that was exactly what I wanted him to say. Because there are no heroics in my picture. These are the survivors of war, and they do what they have to do to stay alive.

You had nursed this project for a long time—did it always have the narrow focus of just the four recruits and the sergeant?

Yes, always. I did not want any overview, to go and see what the generals are doing, no drilling, no flashbacks, no girlfriends, none of that shit. This is the view of a squad in war, nothing else. That's a real *war movie,* you understand? Most pictures of this kind are semi-war pictures. You watch them learn to salute for three months. Hawks made a wonderful picture, a propaganda picture, *Sergeant York,* but only the last twenty percent was World War One. He had seventy-five to eighty percent of the picture take place in Tennessee. I tried to put the war experience on film. I came close. But you can never do it—the only way you could do that and really let the audience feel what it's like is to fire live ammo over the heads of the people in the movie theater.

Would you have preferred to shoot the film on the historical locations rather than in Israel?

No, I'm not concerned about that. The real places don't look the same as they did in 1943. We did shoot some scenes in Ireland and we could have worked in Yugoslavia but there were some last minute problems. Israel had most of the scenery that we were going to need and it worked out very well.

You've said that it was a little weird for you to be using Israeli extras as Nazis.
Yes. All of our Nazi German soldiers wore yarmulkes under their helmets.

Big Red One *went through a traumatic post-production phase and you lost control of it for a time. Are you happy with it in its current form?*
Yes. We shot many things that had to be left out, because the producers would not go for a four, five hour movie, and there is no sense in making a film that no one will show. There was a version that was done by others at one stage, with some things cut and trimmed and then these things were mostly put back in. I'm not talking about length; I'm talking about keeping a scene so it makes sense, so you don't kill the ending, the reason for it. But I am happy with the film as it stands. There are many things left out—but they are all in the book version I did for Bantam.

Do you think you might ever be allowed to restore some of the cut scenes for a complete version for video?
There has been some talk about that. I think it could be done.

How did you become involved with the White Dog *project?*
I was going to make something else. I had a picture lined up at a studio, it was set. And I was asked to see some producers. I told them not to come. I had a deal, I couldn't do anything else. Then my wife told me what the story was: *White Dog.* I choked on my drink. I had read it in *Life Magazine.* Romain Gary, who I knew from when he was a consul in Los Angeles. I loved the story—the first part, not the second. I didn't want to read about Gary's problems with his wife, her suicide. . .

I worked on the story. I changed it a lot. The main thing I kept was the idea of a racist dog. And this was a real thriller, real horror. This wasn't a giant shark going crazy, this was the horror of a *trained* monster—a dog that is trained to attack black people. The way I approached this, the dog is not an animal, it's another character. And I wrote a character of the anthropologist, a black man played by Paul Winfield. And he is a scientist, he doesn't look at the dog emotionally. And this dog is a challenge. How can he reverse what someone has done to that animal? How can he get inside this racist dog's brain without using a knife. And then he loses it for a moment, he becomes emotional.

Did you have any problems getting what you needed from the dog in the picture?

We used several dogs, as you are supposed to do. Each one was best for certain things. And there was a great dog trainer working on the picture.

The film became embroiled in controversy and labeled racist. Can you give me your take on what happened?

We made the picture and the studio brought in a man, a "professional black man" I call him. And he didn't like this story being told. And it was decided that it was better not to show this picture in a big U.S. theater. They were afraid of a riot. And I'd had riots before—*Crimson Kimono*, *Steel Helmet*, they turned over the box office on that. But it was decided that this picture was not safe to be seen in a theatre and it was sold directly to TV. They figured, if there's a riot now it'll be between the family. NBC was supposed to show it but they decided not to because, they said, "It is inappropriate." What kind of word is that? "Inappropriate" is going to your mother's funeral in a jockstrap. But it opened in theaters in Europe. The *London Times* called it a masterpiece. There were no riots.

It seems very deliberately anti-racist. And the black scientist is the most intelligent and sympathetic character in the film.

It was an insult. I have a history of making pro-black, anti-racist films.

After *White Dog* I came to Europe to do some publicity and I was asked to do a picture in France. This gave me a chance to be away from the controversy. I did the picture, in English and French—*Les Voleurs de la Nuit; Thieves After Dark* in English. It was a local subject, but universal. Young people, unemployment, they get in some trouble. I used Bobby Di Cicco from *Big Red One*. A couple of unemployed kids, kind of a *Breathless* situation, but no gangsters. The critics, with some exceptions, murdered me. They didn't like me doing this subject. A lot of them wanted me to bring the underworld into it. I didn't give a damn. I liked it.

And at that time my daughter Samantha was entered in a school here in Paris and we decided to let her stay in school. But we go back and forth. I'm still a visitor. I pay American taxes.

Whose idea was it for you to film Street of No Return? *Are you a fan of David Goodis' work?*

I didn't know it, never read the book before they brought the project to me. But I knew Goodis. We were both in Hollywood after the war. We had both written pretty successful books—I had *The Dark Page*, which Howard Hawks bought, the Warners had bought his *Dark Passage*. I still have the copy he signed for me.

According to his biographer, Goodis had a rather strange private life.

Who doesn't? We were friendly at the time, but I lost touch with him.

He has a very good name in France. I don't know if they still read him in America.

The books are being reprinted now.

A man named Guerif puts the books out in France, and he put me together with the man who owned the movie rights, Jacques Bral. Jacques makes his own movies — but he felt I was right to direct this picture. We worked on a script. The book was good, but there were things that had to be made stronger for the camera. The lead is a singer with a slashed throat. We shot it in Lisbon. The book is set in Philadelphia. Keith Carradine is our lead — I worked with his brother on *Big Red One*. I think it's a good picture.

Can you explain the use of the blackboard and the colors while you're writing a script?

That was something I used to do. I would lay the scenes out on a blackboard, in different colors according to what's happening — white for just telling what happens, red if it's action, blue for romance. If the scene is "Joe meets Lee," that's in white, that's just a meeting. If there's a fight on the bridge, that's in red. And I could use this to gauge the progression. If it's an action story, a thriller, there better be plenty of red for the final act.

I know you've written many scripts that you haven't filmed. Do you write fast?

Yes and no. You can think about a story for years before you go to the typewriter.

Do you do many drafts of a script before you shoot it?

I rewrite certain kinds of stories where I have to be cautious, when I'm on subject matter that's explosive. And sometimes you have to go back and make sure you have what you need to show the progression of a character.

When you're writing a script that you're going to direct, are you already thinking in terms of camera and editing?

Yes. But it's not always written down unless the crew needs to know in advance that a certain kind of equipment is going to be needed.

Generally, at a big studio you have to give them all the details in advance so they can prepare for it. When you are working more independent there is more room to be loose. You invent things as you go along. There are always things that happen between sitting at the typewriter and moving around on the set.

Do you think the direction of the film is as important as the script?

The director is very responsible for many things, of course — but the story is *God*! It doesn't matter the medium. Directing film is something that has been invented in this century, but stories, writing, this has been something important forever—paintings on cave walls, for Christ sake!

Do you have a favorite character of those you created?

The editor in *Park Row*. Everything he says I feel strongly about. He's very close to my heart, that character. This was a composite character, he's not any one actual figure. He's Pulitzer and Bennett and a few others all rolled into one. These were the fighting editors. They owned their papers, you understand, they were responsible for its existence. Today, an editor is not an owner. He has a managing editor over him, and a publisher and a board of directors and maybe a chairman of the board of directors.

Your films are nearly always visually adventurous. What was the impulse that led you to make films in this unconventional style?

You're talking about camera movements and angles and so forth?

Yes.

I am looking for a way to shoot something that will be exciting for the audience, to keep things interesting on the screen. If you've got an exciting story and you present it in a dull way it will be a dull movie. I don't like to shoot a scene from a close angle, medium, long shot, and then take it into the editor and see if we can do anything with it. I want to see the excitement on the set, while we're shooting.

Many of your films contain very long takes. What do you think this adds to the quality of a film?

It's real. You are seeing it as it happens, there's an excitement there. Most films you see, the characters go from an interior to an exterior, there are five cuts, and the exterior is shot two weeks later and the audience can tell. And the actors show it.

How do you think it affects the acting?

With a long take, the actors have got to concentrate more. There's more intensity to the acting—they don't want to make any mistakes if it's a long setup.

The thing that started me understanding that was on *Helmet*. The scene around the Buddha was one shot—the big argument with the communist prisoner and the Japanese American. I got a lot of comments about that.

You have one long take in Forty Guns *that seems to go through the entire town.*

I start with a conversation in a room upstairs. Then we follow him downstairs, more talk, they walk four blocks, stop at an office, come out again, and then Stanwyck rides by with her forty men, all in one shot.

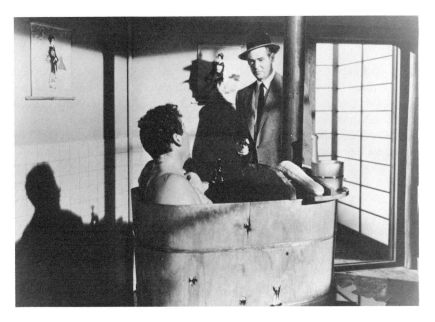

Robert Ryan fills his former "number one boy" full of lead over a misunderstanding in *House of Bamboo* (1955).

My other favorite is in *Park Row*. The camera goes from the saloon to the street to the newspaper office, outside again and into another set, and there's a fight in between. I had three interiors and one exterior in one shot. And that wasn't too easy. No zoom or anything.

And live sound?
Yes. They were wired with their own mikes — it was an experiment. And we had a problem with these mikes that was kind of funny. We had Gene Evans playing the editor and Steve Brody played by George O'Hanlon. And they start fighting, knocking over the first newsstands ever seen in New York. And the actor began to smoke . . . smoke was coming out of him. Something went wrong with the wire for his mike and he was smoking and they had to pour water over him. And the actor was very afraid that he was going to be electrocuted. "Jesus," he said, "what a goddamn way to make a living." I had the same problem with Cameron Mitchell when we were doing *House of Bamboo*. I had a scene of him in a barrel, he's taking a bath. And Ryan comes in and shoots him — two, four, five times, and bullets go through the bathtub and water and blood pour out of the holes. And when Cameron Mitchell climbed into the water, he saw all these wires connected for the bullets to go off. And when anybody sees water and electric wires they don't want to go in the water.

What changes do you foresee in the moviemaking of the future?

It will be so changed you can't imagine how different it will be. The satellite communications, where the whole world can watch something at the same time—this is just the little baby of what there will be. There will be audiences linked together in space, other planets—beyond Saturn and Venus, because you don't think we're the only ones around, do you? And the communications will be so advanced that the kids will learn more than we could ever know and they will learn it all in a week. And movies will be available to each person's exact emotions and needs, whatever he wants available at that moment, instantly created—stories, biographies, pornography. There will be five hundred billion movies available. It will be just great for moviemakers!

Are you optimistics about the future in general?

Very optimistic. I'm very optimistic about what's going to happen to this world. Look, the ways things have gone so far it can only get better...

The Films

With *I Shot Jesse James* (1948), Samuel Fuller made a strong and idiosyncratic directorial debut. Shot in a week-and-a-half on a small budget, made up largely of conversations in cramped interiors, the film is nonetheless invested with what would be a characteristic aura of deliriousness and use of camera and cutting as jarring, cinematic weapons. The unsympathetic hero, his psychological dislocation, the themes of betrayal, jealousy, love begetting violence — staples of Fuller's world in the years ahead — are all crammed into this strange, morbid movie.

Originally hoping to do a film about Cassius and the murder of Caesar (nixed by the producer, Robert Lippert, who did not want to make a movie with "men in bedsheets"), Fuller turned instead to what was, after the shooting at Ford's Theatre, the most notorious assassination in American history, the killing of Jesse James by a shot in the back fired by his friend and gang member Robert Ford. The Jesse James folklore had been perpetuated in Nunnally Johnson's romanticized film of 1939, starring Tyrone Power, and in an equally rose-colored sequel, *The Return of Frank James,* in both of which the "dirty little coward" was played with sniveling villainy by John Carradine. Fuller makes Ford the focus of his film, and dramatizes the degradation that follows the character's Judas-like murder of Jesse. Tired of being always on the run or hiding in the shadows, and lovesick for an actress with conventional ideas about outlawry, Ford is lured by the government's offer of $10,000 and amnesty for anyone who turns in Jesse, dead or alive. The aftermath of the murder is a travesty of his expectations — he lands in jail for a time, receives a fraction of the reward money, and is reviled by everyone, including his fiancée, as treacherous scum. Taking a job as a performer in a stage act recreating the killing, Ford is haunted by the memory of what he did and flees the stage. After various jealous and humiliating encounters with Cynthy, the woman he still hopes to marry, and enigmatic run-ins with a man named Kelley, Ford joins a Colorado silver rush. Teaming up with an old prospector named Soapy, Ford strikes it rich. But ultimately, the fits and starts of his shattered psychological makeup lead to a pointless showdown with Kelley. Dying in Cynthy's arms, Ford fixates again on the long-ago betrayal: "I'm sorry for what I done to Jess ... I loved him."

As Fuller has indicated, *I Shot Jesse James* is a deliberate non–horse opera, an anti-western. In this it was following a trend, not creating one, since Hollywood had been turning out grim and "psychological" westerns with increasing frequency since the war. In any case, Fuller ignores the genre's historical and mythological contexts, concentrating on his characters with a playwright's intensity. This, however, is a matter of the theater's physical scope and a dependence on dialogue. The film does not otherwise perform like a "well-made play" by any means, but lurches chaotically through inexplicable plot developments and unmotivated relationships. The reappearing Preston Foster character, Kelley, the business with the stolen ring, and the state of mind of Cynthy from scene to scene all convey an atmosphere not dissimilar to one of Luis Buñuel's dream-states. This feeling is certainly aided by the somewhat catatonic performing of most of the actors, even the veteran Foster. But John Ireland, as Bob Ford, is quirkily effective, portraying a young, sensuous, and—no denying it—halfwitted "hero." Bob is a lazy sociopath, able to concentrate on just one idea or emotion at a time, and with no thought of the consequences of any act he commits. Beyond Ford's need for amnesty and the cash to settle down with a bride, Fuller indicates a psychological basis for betrayal—"No one loves a man who he fears"—and the scene of Jesse luxuriating in a bath while Ford lugs in hot water buckets and is ordered to scrub his back indicates Ford's servile status in his "friendship" with the celebrated and admired Jesse James. But no sense of deeper motivation is ever really perceived by Ford himself. From beginning to end, including his dying last words, Fuller's Bob Ford behaves with a dazed lack of insight. Whether fully intentional or not, Fuller's murky character study seems finally to say, *Who knows* what makes people do things?

Strangely, Fuller's own comments about Jesse and Bob do not jibe with his film on the subject. While he has described Jesse James as a treacherous transvestite murderer and expressed admiration for the man who killed him, Fuller's dramatization of the story presents a different, more conventional characterization. Jesse, played by a bearded, solemn-voiced Reed Hadley, is Lincolnesque in appearance, wise and decent, well loved by his salt-of-the-earth wife. Bob Ford, in contrast, is introduced in the film as inept and dependent, dropping and losing the money the gang has just robbed from the bank, and having his life saved by Jesse. Ford's behavior following the murder of Jesse is a series of masochistic humiliations and outbursts of violence. True, Fuller stands outside Ford's ugly behavior without condemning him, but this is not exactly an endorsement.

Andrew Sarris has written that Fuller's first film was "constructed almost entirely in closeups of an oppressive intensity the cinema had not experienced since Dreyer's *The Passion of Joan of Arc*." This would appear written more from emotion than fact, since most of the film is actually shot in more conventional medium shots on small, flatly lit sets, much like any average

The "dirty little coward" gets his at the conclusion of *I Shot Jesse James* (1949).

half-hour western series on television in the 1950s. But Fuller does repeatedly resort to extreme closeups, cutting to them abruptly at moments of crisis or verbal violence, using them like a cinematic equivalent of an exclamation mark. It is probably the only "showy" technique that was available on the film's tight budget, but it already shows Fuller's desire to ignore the typically seamless style of Hollywood filmmaking and create his own individual and aggressive cinematic grammar. It is for this small breaking of the stylistic rules, and Fuller's choice of such a raggedly unpredictable, psychologically distraught, and unpleasant protagonist that *I Shot Jesse James* could be seen as the work of a new filmmaker worth keeping an eye on.

For his second film, *The Baron of Arizona* (1949), Fuller returned to the historical West with the fact-based story of James Addison Reavis, a nineteenth century con man and forger whose elaborately faked documents gave Reavis and his Mexican ward, renamed Sophia, ownership of the Territory of Arizona. Fuller details Reavis' complex preparations for his incredible con, a painstaking odyssey through the monasteries and libraries of Spain and Mexico, creating whole dynasties and ancient-looking paper trails that will appear to ratify the legality of his grandiose claims. A flummoxed American government is forced to acknowledge his rights, and Reavis and his ward — now his wife — assume the baronage. His regal fling is short-lived. Reavis' fraud is exposed, he is nearly lynched, and he ends up serving a lengthy prison sentence. In the end, Reavis comes to realize that his feelings for

Sophia transcend his megalomania, and in the end her love is all that remains from this outlandish adventure.

For all of its fascinating, factual story, the heart of the film is the Loli-taesque relationship between the worldly, middle-aged and evil-intentioned Reavis, and the innocent, devoted Mexican waif he raises to be his wife. Fuller has said that the "incestuous" situation was what interested him in the story, but that he had had to "soft pedal" it to get it past the censors. This perverse affair becomes profound, again anticipating *Lolita*, with a coldly ex-ploitative guardian turning into a deeply loving one—"Arizona seems so small," Reavis tells Sophia late in the film, "you seem so great." Finally their positions reverse themselves: Reavis is broken and weeping, Sophia worldly wise and in charge of their future together. "True love" finds itself through a morass of deceit, exploitation, crime, violence and punishment—Fuller's version of a fine romance. Interestingly, though, Fuller's happy ending, rueful as it is, rejects the more downbeat facts of the story. In real life, Reavis was abandoned by his wife and children when he went to prison, and lived his final years in a shack, penniless and alone.

With his second film, Fuller's direction is much more assured. Although the scope of the project would seem to demand a DeMille schedule, Fuller shot it all in 15 days, and got every penny out of a minimal budget. The acting has none of the wooden, halting feel of *Jesse James*. Ellen Drew, although a bit old for her part, is affecting as Sophia, and the role of Reavis is perfectly contoured to the epicene personality and rich theatricality of Vincent Price. Reed Hadley of the inert expression and radio announcer's voice returns from the first picture, but there is solid support from two reliable character pros, Beulah Bondi and Vladimir Sokoloff, as well as a sizable cast in smaller parts. James Wong Howe provided the rich black-and-white cinematography, a coup in itself. *I Shot Jesse James* introduced Fuller's quirky sensibility; *Baron of Arizona* proved he had, as well, the technical and organizational skills to turn out a solid, entertaining and economical movie. It is surprising that the big studio offers did not follow its release; that would have to wait for Fuller's third film, a sensation that no one in Hollywood could ignore.

The Steel Helmet (1950) is decisive on many fronts. It is Fuller's first use of contemporary subject matter, and moreover it is a *scoop*, "torn from the headlines" as they used to say: the first film about the then-raging and controversial war in Korea. It is the first time he uses characters and perspec-tives taken directly from his own personal experience. It is the first time Fuller uses film as a didactic forum, engaging his characters in lengthy moral and philosophical debate. It is Fuller's first truly personal film, and truly groundbreaking as such, for a low-budget, action genre, Hollywood produc-tion.

The Steel Helmet opens on the scene of a massacre. The credits play over a U.S. soldier's helmet with a bullet dent in it. The helmet moves; the

Vladimir Sokoloff and Ellen Drew flanking Vincent Price as the man who would be *The Baron of Arizona* (1950).

sergeant it belongs to has survived, the only survivor from his entire platoon. The sergeant, Zack, is attended to by a Korean War orphan he calls Short Round. Zack is a pragmatic loner and doesn't take kindly to the boy's attachment to him. He wants to send the boy packing with a gift of chocolate for saving his life, but he is all out of chocolate. Short Round tags after him, explaining, "When you save someone's life his heart is in your hands." Zack replies, "You can come along but you're on your own." They come upon a lost patrol wandering in steaming jungle, targets for snipers hidden in the trees. Zack has contempt for the patrol's inexperienced and by-the-book lieutenant, but agrees to lead them to a certain Buddhist temple in exchange for a box of cigars. At the temple, the audience meets each member of the multi-ethnic and eccentric group that includes an Asian, a black, a man who has prematurely lost every hair on his head, and one who has taken a vow of

Varied faces of war in *The Steel Helmet* (1951).

silence. A North Korean officer, hiding within the temple, kills the silent
muleteer and is taken prisoner. The communist major tries to undermine the
squad's belief in their duty, with little success. When Short Round is killed
by a sniper, the major mocks his death and a suddenly enraged Zack shoots
and kills him. The temple comes under a full-scale attack. The lieutenant is
killed in battle, and as a gesture of respect Sergeant Zack adorns his grave
with his "lucky" bullet-scarred helmet. Then Zack and the three survivors
begin the journey to home base.

Shot in a mere ten days — two-thirds the shooting schedule of Fuller's
previous film — with just one set and a half-day of exteriors in Griffith Park
in Los Angeles, *The Steel Helmet* is a remarkable achievement, filled to over-
flowing with its unique, intense mix of violence, symbolism, offbeat characterization and hardboiled discourse. The basic situation, the small outfit cut
off behind enemy lines, biding their time until a bloody last stand, had been
done more than once — in *Bataan, Sahara,* and most notably John Ford's *The
Lost Patrol* — and the melting pot squad, typically containing one immigrant's
son, one country bumpkin, one brassy Brooklynite, was a Hollywood war
movie cliché from at least two wars back. But Fuller retools the shopworn
elements in his own image of war, giving those elements a critical edge and
a dynamic abrasiveness.

His protagonist, Sergeant Zack (played with snarling gusto by Gene
Evans), is a callous, self-centered brute, a spit in the eye to all of those

benevolent, big-brother movie sergeants. He shows zero concern for the young orphan who has just saved his life. When the patrol discovers a dead American off the trail, the lieutenant wants the body properly identified and Zack barks, "Leave him. A dead man is a dead man, nobody cares." Zack is oblivious to the goals of the mission, of the war itself, responsive only to his own immediate needs for survival, food, a box of cigars. He mocks the rituals and proprieties of warfare. But Zack is not necessarily a self-made monster. He has more likely adapted to his situation. War is brutal, Fuller says, and only the brutes are equipped to survive it. Zack's callousness serves a practical purpose. The dead GI's body turns out to be booby-trapped and blows up the soldier sent to collect the dogtags; Short Round, who refuses to go away when Zack tells him, ends up killed. Zack's racism, Fuller implies, is mean-spirited but surface-deep, an offensive defense mechanism, unlike the quiet prejudice of the mild-mannered lieutenant, which clouds his judgment. When Lieutenant Driscoll ignores the advice of Sergeant Tanaka, Zack says they would listen to Tanaka "if his eyes weren't slanted the wrong way." Zack is Fuller's representative of common sense *in extremis.*

Fuller's unlovable heroes are partly a matter of his deliberate pursuit of the anti-cliché, but they are more importantly reflections of his view of life as inherently grey, anarchic, with good and evil churning and intertwined. He has been accused of militarism, jingoism and racism, but these accusations are belied by what is on screen. Fuller's military men are almost always deeply flawed, ambivalent, or outright crazy — the sergeant here blows his stack and shoots the unarmed prisoner at point blank range. And Fuller's dialogues on America and democracy are far from one-sided rhetoric. The Korean POW, trying to get under the skin of his captors, namely the black medic and Asian sergeant, makes rational and stinging remarks about America's treatment of its own blacks, and the concentration camp internment of Japanese-Americans during World War II. Half a century later, discussions of the Nisei internment and revelations about General Eisenhower's possible mistreatment of prisoners of war are still able to stir up controversy. At the time of *The Steel Helmet,* with blacklisting rampant in Hollywood and the country actually at war, Fuller gave evidence of a brave and potentially suicidal iconoclasm by giving his commie major such powerful anti–American ammunition and by letting his American "hero" act with such cold-blooded brutality.

With his third film, Fuller finds his cinematic voice, melding his writing and directing efforts into one cohesive effort. It is the first time Fuller's direction *matters* — if his script had been directed by someone else it would likely have been a very different film, with the quirky and controversial rough edges softened by a more conventional and less "involved" talent, and the film's alleged "talkiness," Fuller's penchant for lengthy verbal debate and anecdote, also cut and tamed. Fuller's first two films were westerns, and it is clearly the contemporary and military background of *The Steel Helmet* that intensified Fuller's handling of the material. He had been in uniform, had been in combat, and came to make his first war movie with a head and a gut full of original thoughts and experiences of war as it really was; he was a reporter with an "exclusive." And Fuller delivered, infusing the film with a unique perspective that was neither the gung-ho heroism of straight-action or propaganda pictures, nor the pious humanism of anti-war movies.

Still working on a low budget and short schedule, Fuller had not yet polished his directing to match the originality of his writing, but with *The Steel Helmet*, the potential of his abilities on the floor became much more apparent. He staged scenes and used actors with a new dynamism, and brought scripted conceptions to vivid fruition. He and his actors handled the film's most memorable moments with perfect emphasis and timing, creating movie epiphanies not easily forgotten: Joe the "mute" speaking for the first time, in agony, when he is knifed in the back; Zack screaming at the mortally wounded major, "If you die, I'll kill you!"; the atheist North Korean prisoner asking for a prayer in the moment before he dies and the medic, playing priest, tapping his head, saying, "Buddha blesses you."

After the huge, unexpected success of *The Steel Helmet*, Fuller was hired by 20th Century–Fox. His first film for the studio, *Fixed Bayonets* (1951), seems an obvious attempt by Darryl Zanuck to grab some of the *Steel Helmet* gold for Fox. It repeats *Helmet*'s war zone (Korea), star (Gene Evans, though Fox contract actor Richard Basehart is the ostensible leading man), concentrated setting (a snowbound cave this time), and brutal violence, although the big studio imprimatur disallowed any repeat of *Helmet*'s disputations about politics/religion/race. *Fixed Bayonets* is a much more naturalistic work, a grunt's-eye view of war as dirty, uncomfortable and dangerous manual labor. Fuller's platoon is made up of tough, brave men, but not heroes—they only do what they are ordered to do, or what they must do to stay alive. Fuller strips his warriors of glamor and sex appeal: they are wet, cold, homely, unshaven. They dream of dry socks, get their ears shot clean off, or are blown to smithereens as they scramble across the icy mountainside like frightened spiders. The men freeze and bleed and die, not in some legendary battle but while doing the "dirtiest" job in combat, a rear guard action, delaying the enemy while the regiment retreats.

Fixed Bayonets is the least didactic of Fuller's war films, and the least self-conscious. Instead of the monologues and bizarre character tags of *The Steel Helmet*, characterization here is done with a kind of pointillist technique that makes one identify more with the squad as a whole than with any individual in it. Only Gene Evans' veteran Sgt. Rock ("an old dogface who's bellied from Tunisia to Czechoslovakia") and Basehart's Corporal Denno, the very reluctant platoon leader, are limned in greater detail, but neither distracts from

Richard Basehart taking aim in *Fixed Bayonets* (1951).

the democratic focus on the group. The film is a continual series of deaths and woundings, yet Fuller's writing is so inventive and inspired that each violent event has a changed tone, painful or funny or mysterious, keeping the viewer as disoriented and on edge as the soldiers on screen, never knowing what to expect next. The death of Rock, the indestructible warrior, comes with dumbfounding irony; he catches a ricochet in the gut while sitting quietly in the cave. "I'm dead," he tells Denno with only slightly less than his usual gruffness, and dies, completing one of the more stoic expirations in film history. Moments of pain and gore are followed by deadpan comedy, and within the same frame. When Rock gets razzed about "playing footsie" with his own squad at the expense of the others, he points to an object on the ground near where one of his men was just shot: "See that? It's Jonesey's *ear!*" The soldiers, properly abashed, stare at the off-screen object for a long moment until one mutters mindlessly, "So that's Jonesey's ear. . ."

All but the opening and closing minutes of the film are confined to the rear guard encampment, a damp cave and the barren rim of a mountain pass. All of it was shot indoors on a Fox found stage, with the hollow sound of an enclosed set. But Fuller manages to give it the feel of something much grander, with his majestically sweeping camera crane and frequent display of bone-shattering firepower, explosions so strong and close by that they seem to jar the lens out of the camera. With the Fox technical apparatus at his command, even though confined indoors, and his largest (still relatively modest) budget and shooting schedule, Fuller begins to indulge his taste for visual flourishes. When Rock storms out of the cave, down the hill, up another, attacking and killing a Korean sniper and returning to his cave, Fuller's airborne camera films the whole sequence in one take, not decreasing the excitement as its looming shadow moves across the background. Fuller shoots the scene of the inexperienced medic cutting a bullet out of his own leg with a full 360 degree pan around the cave, catching each soldier's astonished expression and returning to the medic just as he finishes scraping the lead from his own flesh. Rising to his feet, he cries out with a grotesque mix of shock and pride, "I didn't know I could handle a wound! I'm a surgeon!" A great payoff for a tense, dazzlingly staged scene, but Fuller has a topper before the shot fades, a soldier's off-screen voice piping in with jaded aplomb: "Okay, Wheeler, then come over here and give *me* one of those knife jobs..."

Park Row (1952) is a love letter to Fuller's first infatuation, the newspaper business. Although he surely would have accepted outside financing (on his own terms — Fox supposedly wanted Fuller to do a musical version), it is entirely appropriate that this very personal project was funded by its creator. Fuller took the fortune he had made from his *Steel Helmet* percentage — leaving only "cigar money" — and spent it all to make *Park Row* without interference. He lost every cent.

The film is set at the end of the nineteenth century, and almost all of the action takes place on the titular street in Lower Manhattan, a tumultuous neighborhood between the Bowery and the Brooklyn Bridge, where Fuller himself had worked as a copy boy and young reporter. Fuller treats the creation of modern American journalism as folklore rather than history. Facts mingle with legends, characters are composites of real-life figures, the events of an era are telescoped into one seemingly nonstop, interlocking series of highlights. Fuller is determined to put in as many milestones as he can fit — the invention of the linotype machine, the first newsstand, the funding of the Statue of Liberty, and even such minor Lower Manhattan lore as Steve Brodie's jump off the Brooklyn Bridge — without ever interrupting or slowing down his story. Indeed, his script is so tightly written that every barroom brawl seems to lead directly to another great moment in journalism. And Fuller's direction of the material is equally hectic, creating a veritable *Front Page* in period costume.

Gene Evans, in his third and final lead role for Fuller, plays reporter-turned-editor Phineas Mitchell with his usual vigor. Fuller keeps Evans at high pitch of growling agitation, and the actor is probably not at his most comfortable in his 1880s costume of sideburns, derby and close-cut suits, but he warms to the role and his performance grows in force and understanding as the film goes on. Mary Welch, his co-star, is considerably less successful

Editor Gene Evans bestows a beating on a rival paper's thug. From *Park Row* (1952).

as Charity Hackett, the scheming lady news baron who fires Mitchell, wages a circulation war against him, and ultimately falls for him. Acting in a floridly brittle style, full of whiny sarcasm and much eyebrow-raising, she is cursed as well with a physical homeliness—she bears more than a passing resemblance to Ozark comedienne Judy Canova—that makes the romantic subplot inadvertently terrifying.

Fuller built an entire street for his *Park Row* set, and the film makes full use of it. Interior scenes are often shot with the street visible through windows, with people, horses and wagons passing into view, making the street and its flow of traffic an almost constant presence in the story. Fuller uses these integrated interiors and exteriors even more dramatically in complex traveling one-takes for which the director would become noted. The most amazing of these begins *in medias res* as Mitchell hears that his news wagons are being attacked—he immediately charges from the saloon into the street, fights with four thugs, forces his way into the tidy offices of Hackett's *Star* for a short verbal confrontation, returns to the street, enters the untidy headquarters of his own paper, *The Globe*, fires off their next headline attacking *The Star* ("The Globe Fights with News Not Knuckles!"), and learns that their young newsboy, Rusty, has been put in the hospital by a *Star* henchman. The take ends with Mitchell hearing the name of the attacker and barking, "Get him!" Other directors—Murnau, Welles, Sturges and Ophuls among them—have made notably lengthy moving camera shots, but such set-pieces have tended to be evenly paced, the camera moving at a uniform speed and distance from the action. But here, Fuller's camera is constantly changing speed and perspective, hurtling just ahead of the action like a hand-held newsreel camera one moment, swinging across the street for a distant bystander's viewpoint the next, closing in for medium shots when the dialogue begins and, finally, tightening on a closeup of Evans for the conclusion. Most directors would likely follow such a breathless tour-de-force with a more quietly staged scene, but Fuller operates at an entirely different energy level from most. When Evans barks "Get him!" his closeup flies off the screen in a wipe, replaced by another hurtling tracking shot of the *Star* thug being tossed across the frame into Phineas Mitchell's fist. Mitchell slugs him out to the street, the camera running ahead, just managing to avoid the lurching bodies. The numerous sweeping camera movements are finally halted with a series of fast cuts that come like blows from a blunt instrument as Evans pounds the thug's skull against a statue of Benjamin Franklin, each cut bringing us closer and closer to the brutal impact.

Park Row is a self-indulgent movie. Fuller has made no compromise with his own unquestioning love of the film's subject matter. Mitchell, the crusading newspaper editor, is a noble, unflawed idealist, the journalistic equivalent of the sort of superhero Fuller normally abhors. Mitchell may waver, lose his temper or admit defeat, but his motives are always pure. Newspaper journalism would seem above all a perfect setting for Fuller's brand of black humor and ambiguous heroism, but the foundation of *The Globe* is treated with the reverence usually reserved for stories of the *nation's* founding fathers. The era of the powerful, crusading newspapers that *Park Row* heralds—with such events as the Hearst papers' crusade for the Spanish-American War—was something of a mixed blessing, and the film's climactic funding of the Statue of Liberty allows no implication that such fundraisers are usually cynically jingoistic circulation boosters. This rosy—and for Fuller quite unusual—idealism aside, however, it is his passionate feeling for this material, matched by his furiously physical directorial style, that makes *Park Row* a unique and extraordinary achievement.

Fuller returned to 20th Century–Fox to make *Pickup on South Street* (1953), a small-scale, richly detailed, relentlessly driven narrative, filled with raw energy and imagination. It is perhaps Fuller's most perfectly realized film and one of the undeniable masterworks of the entire crime movie and *noir* traditions. Set in the lower depths of Lower Manhattan—South Street is a stone's throw from Park Row—*Pickup* presents its characters and setting with a pared-down, microcosmic efficiency. It relies on a mere handful of characters (pickpocket, hooker, police informant, sweat-stained precinct captain) and studio sets (subway car and platform, police station, waterfront shack) to evoke the flavor of a teeming Dickensian underworld. The film was

Thelma Ritter, selling names to Murvyn Vye in *Pickup on South Street* (1953).

a medium-budgeted "A" production with a star at the crest of his career in Richard Widmark, and high-priced support from Jean Peters and Thelma Ritter, but Fuller's writing and directing are still at the intense pitch of a ten-day shooting schedule.

Pickup has been derided for its choice of Cold War villains, even called a "McCarthyite tract," as if the film could be lumped together with right-wing Red Menace epics of the period such as *My Son John, Big Jim McClain,* or Howard Hughes' *The Woman on Pier 13* (aka *I Married a Communist*). This is an inept reading of one of the most iconoclastic films in the history of big-studio Hollywood; a true McCarthyite tract was John Wayne's portrayal of Jim McClain as a noble investigator for the noble House Un-American Activities Committee. Widmark's Skip McCoy is a seedy pickpocket, sneering at "patriotic eyewash" and willing to sell government secrets to the highest bidder (Zara: "Do you know what treason means?" McCoy: "Who cares!"). When Skip finally turns on the communist agent, beating him savagely, it is out of personal outrage and vengeance. Candy (Peters) and Moe (Ritter)— who says, "What do I know about commies? I know I just don't like 'em,"—

have exactly the instinctual reaction of a majority of Americans at a time when anticommunism had reached fever pitch. Of course Fuller, a radical individualist, was an anticommunist, but his view of democracy was equally antipropagandist, focusing on the warts and callouses of an America populated by society's dregs.

Widmark is the perfect Fuller "hero," at the height of his leading man phase yet only a few years away from his villainous debut as Tommy Udo in *Kiss of Death*, the cackling psycho who kills an old lady in a wheelchair. Oozing serpentine charm and a cocksure narcissism, Widmark's Skip McCoy is as happy as a clam with his place in the world, able to talk back to cops and enjoy a cold beer in a damp hammock. Who could ask for anything more? his self-satisfied leer seems to ask. Ritter's Moe is Skip 30 years down the road, another jaunty character living by her wits on the criminal fringe, but this one no longer carefree; she is seen weary and depressed in her one-room Bowery apartment, agitated with the fear that she won't have enough money to be buried in a decent cemetery. A haunting scene — and a rebuke to those who think Fuller incapable of subtlety — follows Moe's murder, as Skip retrieves her coffin from a tug en route to Potter's Field, the city cemetery for those who die poor and alone. In view of some critics' attempts to categorize the film as reactionary, it is worth noting that while it is the communist agent who actually kills Moe, it is life on the lonely edges of capitalist America that has brought her to a state of suicidal resignation.

Working for the first time with cinematographer Joe MacDonald, whose previous credits included *The Dark Corner* and *Call Northside 777*, Fuller here uses various scenic elements of the *noir* style but keeps the pace too fast and the narrative too compressed for the painterly lushness and moody slow motion of a classic *noir* look. At the same time, the Fox "house style" watchdogs may have kept Fuller from the full exercise of his own exuberant and experimental stylistics. He contents himself with sudden cinematic grace notes like the crane shot that swoops ahead of Widmark as he swings across the river on a hook, or the way the camera becomes an excited participant as Richard Kiley begins beating Jean Peters across the room. Even without the usual show-stopping stagings, though, *Pickup* is the evident work of a master of the medium, in complete control of all elements. *Pickup* is endlessly inventive and energetic, tightly and efficiently constructed, firmly in the big studio tradition and yet chock-full of distinctive quirks, fresh images and unexpected poetry.

Hell and High Water (1954) begins and ends with a nuclear mushroom cloud. The opening narration declares what follows to be "the story of an explosion," an apt and promising premise for a Fuller movie, but the film turns out to be one of his least lively. It was a studio project, with a script already written by Jesse Lasky, Jr. (Fuller did a revision and got co-script credit), when Fuller came on board. The film was one of the early Cinemascope features and, according to the director, Fox thought Fuller could get away from the static staginess of the first widescreen releases. The film is shot without the sort of reverence for the new frame ratio that was evident in *The Robe* and others, with camera movements and closeups, and shots framed with great spaces of black, but *Hell* is lacking any of the wild inventiveness and true sense of scope of Fuller's later widescreen compositions.

For a film that seems conceived as a grand-scale adventure tale, with foreign settings, sea battles and atomic bombs, it seems to have been produced hurriedly and on the cheap. Well over half the footage is of cramped sound stages representing the interior of a submerged submarine. There is a half-finished quality to the production. The ending is unsatisfyingly abrupt and inconclusive, the submarine still at sea, in enemy waters. Characters run through the film without ever being given anything to do. David Wayne and Gene Evans, both of whom had played lead roles in this period, have virtual bit parts. Perhaps Fox felt it would make the film seem "bigger" to toss a couple more recognizable faces into the cast, even in non-roles, but why didn't Fuller, a fast and inventive writer, give them something to do? Certainly these two skilled character actors should have been spared some of the screen time devoted to the film's leading lady, the notorious Bella Darvi. A mistress of Darryl Zanuck, she was the supposed protégée of both Darryl and his wife Virginia, from whom she derived her new screen name—"Dar" for Darryl, "vi" for Virginia (and, as Jesse Lasky, Jr. quipped, "'Bella' for Lugosi"). She was by no means the worst actress to pass before a movie camera, but her lengthy speeches here, in strangled attempts at English, bring the film to a complete standstill.

Hell does have its high points, including a suspenseful hide-and-seek submarine chase and a moment of stunning, visceral and very Fullerian violence when Victor Francen's scientist gets his finger caught in the hatch as the sub submerges and Richard Widmark's sub captain must jump in and slice the finger off with a knife. Other than these scenes, *Hell and High Water* is a humdrum affair, and the only real failure from Fuller's tenure at Fox.

House of Bamboo (1955) is ostensibly a remake of Harry Kleiner's *Street with No Name*, one of Fox's "neorealist-*noir*" crime dramas from the late 1940s, re-tooled for the era of Cinemascope, color and exotic location shooting (in this case Japan; it was the first Hollywood movie shot there). The original material was appropriate for Fuller with its story of sanctified betrayal and its detailed violence, and *House of Bamboo* adds several more layers of Fullerian themes and preoccupations—Oriental culture, sexual exploitation, interracial romance, and the military. The business of the gang of ex-servicemen planning crimes like military operations actually comes from an unproduced screenplay Fuller wrote just after his postwar return to Hollywood. The mix of elements produces one of the most unusual and most elegantly pictorial gangster movies ever made, with stunning photography and location work.

Following the general structure of *Street with No Name, Bamboo* tells the story of a military policeman infiltrating a criminal gang of nattily dressed Americans living in a Japan still occupied by the U.S. army. Pretending to be Eddie Spanier, a down-and-out thug, Robert Stack's cop comes to the attention of Sandy (Robert Ryan), a gang leader well on his way to building a criminal empire. Recruited into the gang, Eddie becomes the new favorite of Sandy, displacing previous "ichiban" Cameron Mitchell, and during a robbery shootout Sandy saves Eddie, disobeying his own rigid rule that anyone wounded must be killed. The decision to save the wounded Eddie seals Sandy's fate. Collaborating with Mariko (Shirley Yamaguchi), the widow of a man Sandy left for dead, Eddie alerts the authorities to an upcoming caper. Sandy finds out it's a trap and aborts the robbery. When he finally does realize that Eddie is the "spy," Sandy tries to have him killed but the plan is botched and leads to the final chase and shootout on a rooftop amusement park Ferris wheel high over Tokyo.

House of Bamboo is above all an aesthetic pleasure, a feast for the eyes from the opening train robbery with Mt. Fuji as a backdrop to the breathlessly vertiginous climax, a sumptuous combination of Joe MacDonald's exquisite photography (which works particular wonders with shiny red objects) and Fuller's exuberant and adventurous stagings. The director uses the Cinemascope camera here as the studio had supposedly asked him to do on *Hell and High Water*. While other directors at the time complained of the new frame ratio ("Good only for snakes and funerals," Fritz Lang said), Fuller unleashes its potential with lightning fast tracking shots, disorienting setups (the overhead view of the dying gangster on the operating table), bizarre compositions (Mt. Fuji framed by the splayed feet of a corpse) and dazzling panoramas as he hoists the camera to various lofty bird's-eye views.

The film's preoccupation with betrayal is endlessly advanced. Deceivers and spies are everywhere: Mariko has kept her marriage a secret, the gangster Eddie is really a policeman, the dignified Mariko pretends to be a cheap "kimono girl," a newspaperman informs on the police to Sandy, Sandy believes Mariko to be cheating on Eddie with another American, Sandy wrongly executes Griff, his loyal "Number One Boy," and a traditional Japanese dance troupe turns into a bunch of swing-band jitterbugs. The effect is a rich web of duplicity.

Fuller's interest in interracial relationships and cross-cultural tensions is explored in the romance of Mariko and Eddie. Typically, he reverses the stereotypical treatment of this situation and shows societal disapproval from a perspective outside that of the white Westerner. In a part that could easily have been window dressing, Shirley Yamaguchi's Mariko is a complex character, an active participant in Robert Stack's dangerous enterprise, and many scenes, including the charming breakfast-and-bath sequence and the tense moment when she first encounters "Eddie" with Robert Ryan (a

Bella Darvi entertains sailors as the only woman aboard the sub in *Hell and High Water* (1954).

wonderful scene in which she must deal with an array of confusions and a beating), are written from Mariko's point of view. *House of Bamboo*'s complex characterizations, thematic undercurrents and visual splendor are still more evidence of the mislabeling of Fuller as a "primitive."

Run of the Arrow (1957) is Fuller's most elaborate dramatization of his fascination with the meaning of patriotism and national allegiance. O'Meara, the Confederate soldier who has fired the last shot of the Civil War — wounding and then saving the life of Ralph Meeker's Union officer — is violently embittered by the South's humiliation. Rather than become a part of the re–United States, O'Meara turns his back on the country and heads for the frontier lands of the West. He teams up with an old Indian scout, Walking Coyote, and becomes intrigued by Coyote's tribe, the Sioux, learning the tribal language as the pair make their way into Indian country. Waylaid by a band of renegades led by Crazy Wolf, O'Meara and Walking Coyote must make the "Run of the Arrow," a ritualistic chance to run for their lives. The old Indian dies but O'Meara is saved by a Sioux woman, Yellow Moccasin. O'Meara is gradually accepted by the tribe of Yellow Moccasin, whom he marries and he comes to see the Sioux as his only national allegiance. When the Sioux agree to sign a peace treaty with the Americans, O'Meara finds himself caught between two hate-filled elements, on one side Crazy Wolf and

Shirley Yamaguchi in *House of Bamboo* (1955).

on the other the equally renegade Lieutenant Driscoll, the very man O'Meara shot on the last day of the Civil War. After various provocations, the Indians attack the new U.S. fort. O'Meara violates Sioux ritual to save Driscoll from torture, killing him with the same bullet he fired at the film's beginning, and in so doing realizes he has been fooling himself: he is not a Sioux, he is—like it or loathe it—an American. The film concludes with the weary Southerner returning to take his part in the "birth of the United States."

Run of the Arrow is that rare thing in Hollywood, a genuine film of ideas. The central theme of nationalism versus individualism, or, on the personal level, that of self-interest versus responsibility permeates every scene, from blunt and lengthily didactic conversations to the tiniest bits of business and seemingly throwaway lines of dialogue. As usual in Fuller's ambivalent universe, his ideas are provocative not comforting, and the questions raised remain largely unanswered. O'Meara's return to America is no happy ending but a painful reconciliation. O'Meara's problems with his country still exist but he has decided he cannot, after all, run away from them. Fuller emphasizes this dramatic inconclusiveness with one of his characteristic end-title exhortations: "The Ending Can Only Be Written by You."

On a purely technical level, *Run of the Arrow*'s screenplay is a case study in structural strength and density, from the twice-fired "last bullet" to the various other parallels and paradoxes that support and enrich an already strong narrative line. Fuller writes scenes with multiple layers of meaning, embedding ironies within ironies. The second firing of the bullet is an example: O'Meara's different intent in each firing shows his emotional journey from hatred to compassion. The "revived" last bullet of the war he has carried over his heart also represents O'Meara's refusal to accept the war's humiliating conclusion, and its second firing symbolizes his acceptance that the last bullet of the war has, indeed, been discharged. And more: the test of O'Meara's allegiance to the Sioux is his ability to kill an American, but when he *does* kill an American—shooting Driscoll with the last bullet to save him from slow torture—it is in violation of Sioux ritual and ultimately proves O'Meara's deep-seated allegiance to the traditions of America.

Fuller's cast is one of his best, with no fewer than four strong male performers in Rod Steiger, Brian Keith, Ralph Meeker and Charles Bronson. Steiger plays O'Meara with a brooding, prickly heaviness that makes no easy bid for sympathy but earns it nonetheless as his character finds enlightenment. Steiger, however, seems to be trying for some sort of mumbling methodology and a Brandolike idiosyncrasy of accent, and at this he fails miserably, his attempts at varying thick speech patterns ebbing and flowing from scene to scene. Jay C. Flippen as Walking Coyote, ill-served by a Shemp Howard wig, is the only real mistake in a large cast. The character of Yellow Moccasin, however, seems underdeveloped in comparison to Fuller's usual

strongly written female characters—perhaps this had to do with actress
Sarita Montiel's difficulties with English. (This problem was solved by getting
Angie Dickinson to dub her lines in post-production, a similar job perhaps
should have been done to erase Steiger's strangled search for an accent.)

Working for the first of four times with cinematographer Joseph Biroc,
Fuller again shows his skill with photogenic locations, presenting his Utah
landscapes in spacious wide shots and swooping movements of the by-now
inevitable camera crane. These sumptuous images, bright and simple and
precise, contrast with the emotional turmoil and confusion of the hero.

The complex issues Fuller raises, and the many layers of meaning contained within his script, make *Run of the Arrow* a rich and provocative experience even after repeated viewings.

China Gate (1957) is an adventure story set in Vietnam in the year 1954,
"the hottest front in the world," with war raging between the French colonial
rulers and the Russian and Chinese-supported Viet-Minh revolutionaries. A
squad of Foreign Legionnaires journeys behind enemy lines to find and
destroy the communists' main ammo dump. Lucky Legs, a half-caste party
girl and drunkard, known and trusted by the revolutionary soldiers, agrees to
lead the squad in exchange for her young son's evacuation to America. She
doesn't count on the squad including Brock, an "American dynamiter" and
the father of her son. Brock abandoned his wife and son when he learned the
child had Asian facial characteristics. Interpersonal tensions flare up as the
squad makes its way north: Brock and Lucky Legs still love each other, but
Brock cannot overcome his instinctual racism. Reaching the enemy headquarters, Lucky Legs renews her friendship with Major Cham, an ambitious
communist who offers the girl and her son a new life with him when Moscow
makes him chief of a Viet-Minh Politburo. Instead, she kills him and sacri-
fices her life to blow up the ammo dump. Atoning for his past behavior,
Brock goes back to take care of his son.

China Gate opens with newsreel footage and narration giving the background of the Indochina war, and with typically swift, bold strokes Fuller
moves from the historical perspective and crowds of anonymous faces to the
immediate and personal, a single boy and his dog. The narrator intones, just
before the advance of a hungry Vietnamese thug, "All animals have been
eaten . . . all but *one*." (Was Fuller perhaps paying homage to the old tabloid
definition of a newsworthy story, "Man Bites Dog"?) In a bombed-out city
that seems to have not a single interior intact, Fuller's camera makes ma-
jestic, gliding crane shots as it follows the boy back to the roofless bar run by
his mother, Lucky Legs—Angie Dickinson's character, introduced with her
now legendary appendages stretched across the entire Cinemascope screen.

As in his previous "military mission" films, Fuller alternates between
noisy action scenes and quiet—though often emotionally violent—"down-
time" conversations between his diverse and always opinionated characters.

The "run" under way in *Run of the Arrow* (1957).

Aside from indulging Fuller's penchant for didactic debate, these talk sessions serve to put the audience off guard for the next burst of violence. A meandering, comical monologue by Pigalle, the former French traffic cop, lulls the viewer to the point of tedium by the time he concludes, "I tell you, this is the way to *live!*" and is instantly riddled with machine gun fire. Brock's and Lucky Legs's running discourse on racism is bluntly stated, even for Fuller, and many of the lines read like the purple blurbs of a movie poster: "Five years is a long time to think about one woman every night"; "You didn't look like a thirty-buck Chinese bride"; "The only cross he has to carry is his eyes"; "I'm a little of everything and a lot of nothing."

Of all Fuller's films containing Cold War politics, *China Gate* is the one in which he most clearly takes sides, at least tacitly endorsing his Legionnaires' fight "for the whole Western world." The two most sympathetic soldiers—Goldie (Nat King Cole), a black American, and the emotionally disturbed Hungarian refugee—are rabid members of a kind of AntiComintern, and Goldie is given much of Fuller's own military bio (Big Red One, Sicily, Falkenau). Still, the story is not without an ironic perspective on the glories of the "Western world," since one of its representatives, Brock, is a brutal, callous racist, physically repulsed by the thought of his Asian-looking child. And Lucky Legs, the emotional center of the film, is above politics, friendly with both sides of the conflict, betraying the revolutionaries out of maternal concern for her son's future.

Fuller's next film, *Forty Guns* (1957), takes place in the baroque territory first settled by *Duel in the Sun, The Furies* and *Johnny Guitar*—excessive, tempestuous westerns where violence goes hand in glove with sexual hysteria. Fuller's universe was already filled with examples of a brutal intertwining of love, lust and pain, but *Forty Guns* takes the violence/love duality to the frenzied pitch of a fever dream, a Freudian hothouse, where *every* gun is a sex object, where every kiss ends in bloodshed.

En route to California, Griff Bonnell and his brothers Wes and Chico enter Cochise County, the domain of the all-powerful Jessica Drummond. The town is shot up by Brock Drummond, Jessica's young punk brother. Griff, "legal killer," feels forced to intervene and arrest him, but since Jessica owns the town and the judge she has no trouble getting her brother freed. Griff and Jessica meet again when he interrupts a dinner she's having with her "forty guns," and has one of her men arrested. A tense flirtation develops between Drummond and Bonnell and comes to fruition when the two are caught in a violent storm. Sheriff Logan, afraid that his part in various crimes and corruptions will be exposed by Bonnell, and even more anguished by Jessica's infatuation with Griff, hangs himself. Wes, marrying the local gunsmith, is murdered by Brock. Griff arrests young Drummond, causing an inevitable angry rift in his relationship with Jessica. When she goes to visit Brock in jail, he makes a sudden escape, using his sister's body as a shield when Griff approaches him in the street. Griff calmly shoots Jessica, kills Brock, and walks away. Some time later, as Griff rides a wagon out of town, a chastened—and barely healed—Jessica runs after him.

Forty Guns is the Fuller film that is most clearly conceived as a pure cinematic experience. The course of events and the development of the various relationships have no objective reality beyond their filmic existence. Does the story unfold over the course of days, as it seems at times to indicate, or over a period of months, as logic would imply? Ultimately, the story takes place over a period of 80 minutes—the running time of the film. Similarly, a dramatic scene like "The Walk," Griff's legendary unarmed stalking of a perpetrator, is a cinematic concept, not a real one—it exists only as an edited entity, complete with rhythmic cuts, extreme closeups and dramatic music.

To convey his theme of violence and sexual desire, Fuller uses symbols and metaphors with such overwhelming gusto that the film passes beyond self-parody to a loony, over-the-top surrealism. Beginning with the title, the film's gun lust is unrelenting. Stuffed with phalluses, *Forty Guns* is like a casebook on sexual frenzy—written by the patient. A couple flirts as the assorted weapons in a gun shop window shadow their faces. A woman is "built like a 40-40." In a famous shot, an irised view of gunsmith Eve Brent through an open rifle barrel dissolves into a shot of her being kissed.

Gene Barry takes a killing bullet on his wedding day, while brother Barry Sullivan looks on. From *Forty Guns* (1957).

Jessica Drummond's childhood definition of a man is "everything with two feet and a gun." Facing Griff across the dining table, she asks him, "your trademark . . . may I feel it?" To which Griff replies, "Uh-uh, it might go off in your face." When, after the climax where Griff's trademark does "go off" and he shoots her in cold blood, she is told she is a "lucky woman" and that Griff "put that bullet in you right where he wanted to put it," she runs off, apparently feeling very lucky indeed, to catch the Mr. Right who shot her. Not content with letting the assorted weaponry carry all the weight of the nonstop phallic symbolism, Fuller makes Jessica "a woman with a whip," has her make a provocative reference to being "bit by a rattler when I was fifteen," and shows her passion fully unleashed under the churning fury of a cone-shaped "twister." *Forty Guns* is less a story than a state of mind, Jessica Drummond's psychosexual odyssey from unhappy dominant to satisfied submissive. Fuller's framing device is the key: Jessica, on horseback and clad in black, masculine garb, leading forty men ("forty guns") in the opening shot, while in the final image she is in a frilly white dress and on foot, following one man.

The climactic showdown is justly renowned for its iconoclastic originality, another example of Fuller pulling a switch on the expected, sentimental cliché. Jessica's trash brother holds her in front of him, taunting Griff with insanely gleeful confidence: "Let's see you shoot her!" Griff, without a pause, shoots her. Jessica makes an ugly, agonized whimper, sliding from Brock's arms. Griff shoots Brock repeatedly. Griff sinks to his knees, screaming with weird indignation, "I'm killed, Mr. Bonnell, I'm killed!" As brother and sister lie crumpled in the dirt, Griff strides past, muttering to a bystander, "Get a doctor. She'll live."

Verboten (1959) has a "front page" hook—the existence of neo–Nazis in postwar Germany—and one eye on the drive-in Zeitgeist, the marauding Nazi "Werewolves" presented as disaffected juvenile delinquents (the press-kit promises strong appeal to "the millions of today's teenagers who comprise the so-called 'beat' generation!"). But as usual, Fuller conceives the melodramatic material as a vehicle for ideas and recurring themes—infiltration, betrayal and national identity. Furthermore, his didactic impulse is seen here in its most undiluted form, particularly in what amounts to a short film-within-the-film, summing up the Nazi crimes against humanity in a stunning and complex montage that mixes dramatic footage with stock newsreel film of German war criminals and their helpless victims, with a narration read by Fuller himself.

Verboten begins at the very end of World War II, the U.S. Army rolling over the last vestiges of the German resistance. Sgt. Brent, part of a patrol flushing out snipers from a rubble-strewn German town, is wounded by a shot in the buttocks. A German woman, Helga, drags him to safety, nursing his wound and hiding him from the retreating German troops. Helga declares she was "never a Nazi," and Brent eventually agrees, telling her "you're kosher." In love with Helga—and believing she feels the same—Brent arranges to stay on in Germany after the war so he can marry her. Working as a civilian liaison, Brent provides scarce food and goods for Helga and her young brother, Franz, a bitter teenager whose arm was destroyed by an American bomb. Franz falls under the influence of Bruno, an unregenerate Nazi and leader of the "Werewolves," a Himmler-inspired secret "army" that aids escaped war criminals and generally wreaks havoc on the occupying forces. Bruno has also managed to get a day job at the U.S. Army command HQ, allowing him to attack his enemy from within. When Helga takes the unruly Franz to the Nuremberg war trials, the horrifying accomplishments of the Nazis stun him—"I didn't know . . . I didn't know!" he cries—and he sees what Bruno and his ilk really represent. Franz helps bring a quick, violent halt to the activities of the local Werewolf pack.

It is a strange jumble of a movie, fascinating in part because of a chaotic form that jumps around from battle scenes to domestic crises to stark documentary. The central love story is not very compelling. Though very well played by James Best, the character of Brent is weak and hardly forceful (as is perhaps to be expected of a character who is first seen getting shot in the rear) and tends to fade into the background. The dramatic, two-stage climax of the Nazi war crime scene followed by the killing of Bruno doesn't even involve Brent. Fuller gives better lines — and a lot less whining — to the deskbound Captain Harvey, and the dramatic focus of the film is Franz, who goes from Werewolf to free-thinker in one uneasy lesson.

Even for Fuller the film has an unconventional surface: soldiers battling to the rhythms of Beethoven's Fifth, Wagner accompanying an otherwise silent montage of Werewolves on a rampage,* grainy documentary shots recklessly intercut with backlot action, and the aforementioned "documentary," with Fuller reading his own essay/narration. *Verboten's* conceptual boldness could be compared only to Godard, who, of course, derived much of his style from Fuller films like this one.

The Crimson Kimono (1959) shows the writer-director working in a low key. On the surface the film could easily be mistaken for an episode of any average cop show on television. A Fuller film without unusual and creative elements would be almost unimaginable, though, and indeed beneath *Kimono's* conventional-looking cops 'n' criminals surface is a sophisticated love story and an imaginative study of the insidious side of racism.

At an L.A. burlesque house, platinum blonde stripper Sugar Torch finds a stranger with a gun in her dressing room. She runs screaming from the theater and is shot dead in the busy street outside. Charlie Bancroft and Joe Kojaku, police detectives and close friends (they "met in a foxhole") are assigned to the case. The investigation leads them to a painter of Oriental subjects, Christine Downs. Her drawing of the murder suspect gets her shot at, so the detectives bring her to their place for protection. Charlie falls for Chris and begins making plans to marry her. But Chris favors Charlie's Nisei partner, Joe, and he reciprocates her feelings. Violently frustrated by the situation, Joe vents his anger during an exhibition Kendo swordfight, nearly killing Charlie. Neurotically self-conscious about his racial background, Joe believes that his love for a white woman has brought out Charlie's secretly racist feelings about him. But after the Sugar Torch killer is found — it is Roma, a woman who mistakenly believed her lover was involved with the stripper — Joe sees a parallel with his own behavior toward Charlie. He now accepts that Charlie's reaction was caused by simple jealousy and not racism. The friendship remains damaged, however, and Joe and Chris walk away without Charlie.

Contrasted with the stylistic and emotional hysteria of the two previous films, *The Crimson Kimono* is a cool and self-effacing work. Taking a break from his usual raucous, iconoclastic characters, Fuller initially makes Joe and Charlie decent, easygoing guys (adding to the impact of Joe's eventual flareup), and many of the other characters are equally likable and intelligent.

---

*The film's theme song, however, is decidedly non-classical — one of the most unbearably soupy creations ever committed to film.

The *other* bald woman in a Fuller film: a victim of postwar tensions in *Verboten* (1959).

Aside from the brassy opening in which Sugar is murdered on the street, and the later Kendo fight, Fuller keeps away from any flashy pyrotechnics, but this calm, efficient surface actually masks some remarkably fluid and complicated takes, the most impressive of which is the early scene of Joe and Charlie in their hotel suite. In this scene the ease and closeness of their long friendship is evoked by the continuity of the long take, with the camera tracking in and out of rooms as the two men go about their morning routines.

Typically, Fuller shows racism to be the product of an aberrant psychology—in this case, paranoia. Always looking for the unexpected twist, he makes his racist Joe Kojaku the ostensible victim of it. Fuller compounds this irony by surrounding him with a collection of Caucasians all of whom are immersed in Asian culture, from Sugar Torch (with her crimson kimono and karate act) to Chris, Roma, Hansel and Charlie (in whose veins a pint of Joe's Asian blood flows). But racism, which is presented as absurd, is only a red herring in this story. The real theme is stated by Anna Lee's cigar-smoking Mac, the Skid Row muralist: "Love is like a battlefield: somebody has to get a bloody nose."

Fuller's next film, *Underworld U.S.A.* (1961), is an unrelentingly dark and violent gangster movie, with the singlemindedness and fateful circumscription of a Greek tragedy. Young Tolly Devlin, a brutal street thief, and Sandy, a surrogate mother to the boy, see a man being beaten to death in a shadowy alleyway. The man is Tolly's father, a small-time crook. Although he can identify one of the killers as Vic Farrar, the boy refuses to cooperate with the police, preferring to seek vengeance on his own terms. Twenty years of crime and jail time pass before Tolly catches up with a dying Farrar. Tricking Vic into naming the other three killers, Tolly taunts him by withholding forgiveness and slaps him around as he expires. Gela, Smith and Gunther, the other three, are now middle wheels in a huge crime syndicate. Tolly rescues Cuddles, a syndicate moll who has outlived her usefulness, and gets her to squeal on Smith for a murder she saw him commit, thus reserving him a seat in the electric chair and taking care of the second of Tolly's father's killers. Getting a job inside Gela's mob, Tolly cuts a deal with the crusading crime commissioner, Driscoll, and frames Gunther as a traitor. Gus, Gela's efficient young killer, "barbecues" Gunther in a car explosion. Getting to know Connors, the boss of bosses, Devlin concocts another frameup and Gela is shot to death. Cuddles, meanwhile, has fallen hard for Tolly and he decides to get married, have kids, go straight. He refuses Driscoll's request to help put Connors out of business; Tolly's only motive has been personal revenge, not civic duty. But when Connors puts a contract on Cuddles, Tolly kills him, getting mortally wounded in the process. He stumbles through the streets, crumbling in the same dark alley where his father died.

Underworld U.S.A. is an important, pivotal work in the gangster genre. It is the last great work in the classic tradition, the hero's doomed trajectory, the ritualized rubouts, the black-and-white images of glistening, rain-splattered studio streets, the final stumbling death march, all reminiscent of such standards from the 1930s as *Public Enemy, Scarface,* and *The Roaring Twenties.* But *Underworld U.S.A.* also anticipates the cool, corporate-look, suburban gangster films of the 1960s, notably *The Killers* and *Point Blank.* Fuller's gangsters are transitional figures, having gone from being alleyway thugs to tax-paying executives. They have come up from the "underworld" and now reside in mainstream America. Connors, the big boss, holds court at an empty swimming pool, symbolic of the syndicate's antiseptic façade (in fact, the pool is a charitable gift to the community's underprivileged children).

The film has a deliberate, inexorable quality, a consistent darkness and pessimism in its tone and visual style. There is no letup, no moment of humor or calm in these characters' lives. The camerawork is correspondingly tight, airless, full of harsh closeups, with almost none of Fuller's signature traveling crane shots and long takes that connote chaos, life beyond the frame and the sense that "anything can happen." Only one thing can happen to Tolly and the gangsters in *Underworld U.S.A.* The film's final image is typical of its tunnel vision. With Tolly lying in the street, most directors would have slowly craned away, music swelling as the camera rises far above the lonely death scene. Fuller moves *in* for an ugly, frame-filling closeup of Tolly's fingers in a twisted fist, symbol of a life consumed by anger and violence.

Underworld's characters are darker variants on familiar Fuller types. Sandy is another hardboiled mother figure like Moe and Mac, but without the humor and tough insights (although she does have Moe's penchant for foisting neckties on people). Tolly is a spy and betrayer, a triple agent using both the mob and the police to further his own plans for revenge. Like Skip McCoy, who also sneers at righteous crime-fighters, Tolly is motivated only by self-interest. Connors' evil effect on society, like the Communist menace to Skip, makes no difference to Tolly. Only when the crime boss touches him personally, by threatening the life of Cuddles, does Tolly strike out, leaving Connors floating in his swimming pool like a hippo in a bathrobe. Dolores Dorn's Cuddles, whose love eventually humanizes the ice-blooded Tolly, is another familiar figure, but stands out as the saddest and most deeply romantic of Fuller's many bruised-by-life heroines. Her passion is unexpectedly moving. She tells Tolly: "I die inside when you kiss me."

Fuller's next film returned to a wartime setting but differed sharply from his first three war movies, which were all constrained and shaped by their low budgets and concomitant artificial production values — the soundstage "exteriors" representing jungle and mountain pass, the minimal troop strength, the reliance on stock footage. *Steel Helmet* and *Fixed Bayonets* could very nearly be mounted as plays (although the theater would probably be blown to pieces by the end of the first performance). Fuller transcends the lack of verisimilitude through the intensity of his direction, an eye for gritty detail, a way with on-screen violence, and his writer's skills with colorful situations and characters. But these low-budget films allowed the filmmaker no opportunity to exercise the genre's capacity for spectacle. *Merrill's Marauders* (1962), a well-funded production shot entirely in the very authentic jungles and swamps of the Philippines, gave Fuller that opportunity. The resulting movie is narrowly focused yet epic in effect, containing battle scenes of a visual splendor and kinetic excitement comparable to the work of Ford, Kurosawa, Eisenstein, Lean — that is, comparable to the greatest battle scenes ever filmed. It is also a grim and painful war movie, a harrowing depiction of combat's physical and mental toll.

Merrill's Marauders is the true story of a 3,000-man unit that fought behind Japanese lines in Burma in 1944. In the film, fierce fighting and the hellish terrain have brought the soldiers to the edge of collapse, but the high command continues to order them back into combat. Merrill reluctantly lies to his men, promising they will be relieved after one more mission when he knows that they will be kept fighting again and again. He clashes with Stock, a platoon leader and Merrill's surrogate son, who feels his responsibility is to his men while Merrill's is to the inhuman demands of the commanders. A grueling trek across jungle and mountain and a *banzai* attack by the Japanese leave the Marauders in a state of total collapse. Merrill exhorts them to go on, begins struggling ahead himself, and falls dead from heart failure. Stock, inspired, says, "You heard the General." And the remaining soldiers slowly, painfully get to their feet and head for the next battle.

A line supposedly said to Fuller by a Pentagon general in regard to *The Big Red One* is far more applicable to this film: "No recruitment flavor." Regardless of the noble cause behind their mission, the Marauders are presented as being essentially sentenced to death by slow torture. The film is a chronicle of their agonizing depletion by combat, disease and exhaustion. A concluding narration informs viewers that Merrill's 3,000 men were reduced to a mere 100 by the end of the campaign. Merrill's line to the fading troops, "If you can breathe, you can fight," which he means as a spirited challenge, actually defines the Army's attitude towards the Marauders, a conscious decision to work them to death. Merrill himself, aware of his fragile heart condition, is a virtual suicide. Of course, the film could be read as a paean to duty and self-sacrifice. But Fuller doesn't sentimentalize. His soldiers don't talk about the war or the enemy, only about food and going home and staying alive. They fight furiously when they have to, but there is no macho posturing. A startlingly effective scene involves Claude Atkins' tough, burly Sgt. Kolowicz resting on the ground after the battle for Shaduzup. A tiny Burmese boy comes by and rubs his beard and is joined by an old woman who gives the sergeant rice. Kolowicz begins crying uncontrollably. Fuller's harsh vision was apparently softened in two places (presumably by Milton Sperling, the producer and co-writer): the grim ending is tagged with some upbeat stock footage of well-groomed troops on parade and in the fight in the concrete maze (triangular stones built to support fuel tanks), in which Fuller had wanted to show the Americans shooting other Americans, illustrating the panic and confusion of battle. Fuller gets his point across by subtler means. After the fury of the battle a Marauder climbs on top of the stones and the camera makes a 360-degree turn with him as he surveys the dead. The American and enemy bodies are crumpled together, indistinguishable.

Shock Corridor (1963) tells the story of a newspaper reporter, Johnny Barrett, with a plan to solve a murder committed inside an insane asylum. With the reluctant help of his stripper girlfriend, Cathy, Barrett passes himself off as a sex pervert and enters the asylum as a patient. He tries to get information from the three patients who witnessed the murder: Stuart, a Korean War veteran who collaborated with the enemy and now believes he is a Confederate general; Boden, a scientist who helped create the atom bomb and now has the mind of a child; and Trent, a black man who has snapped from the pressure of being a "test case" at a racist Southern university and now

Moments from death, Jeff Chandler exhorts his men to go on. *Merrill's Marauders*
(1962).

imagines he is a vicious Ku Klux Klan bigot. Barrett's investigation does not
go smoothly and he is constantly under assault from the asylum's aggressive
lunatics (including a fanatical opera lover and a locked roomful of nympho-
maniacs). When a riot breaks out, Barrett ends up in a straitjacket and is given
shock treatments. He begins to believe Cathy really is the sister he lusts after.
He regains his normal frame of mind in time to find out from Boden that
Wilkes, a hospital attendant, is the murderer, but before he can use the information his mind snaps again. A hallucinatory thunderstorm in the hospital
corridor brings Barrett back. He beats a confession out of Wilkes, writes up
his story and wins the Pulitzer Prize. But the experience has, in the end, cost
him his sanity.

    Shock Corridor takes Fuller back to the impoverished circumstances
of his early productions. And as before, Fuller uses startling situations and
provocative ideas and intense, even hysterical direction of scenes as his
equivalent for "production values." *Shock Corridor* is hyped-up, unpredictable, grotesque, tasteless, embarrassing and scary—a film about the crazy
that is crazy. It is a film made with a delirious obliviousness to the conventional need for coherence and believability. It is a personal film to an extent

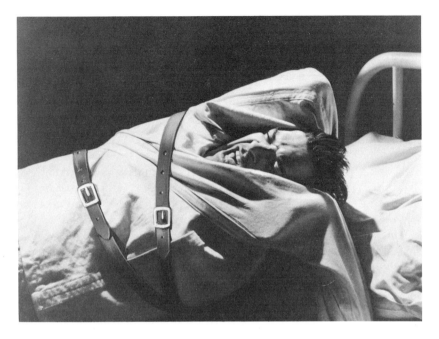

Peter Breck, trying to win a Pulitzer the hard way, in *Shock Corridor* (1963).

rare in the history of commercial Hollywood cinema, not merely in the way the film is conceived as a vehicle for dramatizing Fuller's ideas on a variety of hot topics, but in the way his inimitable tabloid-philosopher's personality is present in every frame of film. That personality, untamed by various proprieties, is what makes *Shock Corridor* alternately electrifying and unbearable. When critics refer to a certain "camp" or unintentionally absurd quality in Fuller's films, it is *Shock Corridor* they most often have in mind. Admirers of the film have difficulty refuting these charges. It *is* absurd. Unreservedly pretentious, it makes its madhouse a metaphor for America, and explores such topics as racism, psychiatry, patriotism, and the creation of the atomic bomb, but it does these things with the bluntness of a superhero comic book. The dialogue comes with undigested exposition ("You've got to be crazy to want to be committed to an insane asylum to solve a murder") and ironies are driven home with a sledgehammer ("What a tragedy — an insane mute will win the Pulitzer Prize!"). An Asian psychiatrist talks like a hardboiled detective, while a stripper has alliterative flights of eloquence ("Do you think I like singing in that sewer with a hot light on my navel?" "You're on a hopped-up show-off stage! Don't be Moses leading your lunatics to the Pulitzer Prize!"). Some scenes are ludicrous to the point of sublimity (most notably, Cathy's feather boa bump-and-grind, and the moment containing Johnny's panicked voiceover cry of "*Nymphos!*"). With such threadbare improvisations as the use of Fuller's own 16mm home movies as "hallucinations" (including shots of the amusement park used in *House of Bamboo*), the film veers dangerously close to Edward Wood, Jr. territory.

For all its nutty gracelessness, however, the film is a triumph, original and audacious. It is a powerful and frightening tour of an America gone mad, a horror movie in which the monster is a nation's destructive energy.

The Naked Kiss (1964) opens with lurid gusto and the most famous scene in any Fuller movie. Looking straight into the lens, a woman (Constance Towers) begins attacking the camera with her purse. In a reverse subjective view we see the man she is beating. The struggle knocks the woman's wig off and reveals that her head is shaved bald. "I'm drunk, Kelly . . . please, I'm drunk!" the man groans, falling to the carpet. The scene opens out to a long low-angle shot of a living room, all crisp greys and precise shadowwork by cinematographer Stanley Cortez. A jazz trumpet is screaming on the sound-track. Kelly, still bald, in black bra and skirt, pummels the man to the ground and then hits him with a blast of seltzer. She pulls out his wallet, counts his money: "Eight hundred dollars! You parasite!" She counts off bills as the man lies whimpering under her. "I'm not rolling you, you drunken leach," she says, "I'm taking only the seventy-five dollars that's coming to me." She stuffs it into her bra, gives him a final kick and moves away. Staring directly into the camera-as-mirror, she puts her wig back in place—and the title comes up on screen, the credits rolling over her fierce stare as she applies her makeup. Kelly rips her photo off the wall and exits, leaving the pimp to retrieve his scattered cash. The prologue ends.

Two years have passed and Kelly, her blonde hair grown back, gets off a bus in the small town of Grantville. Attracting the attention of Griff, the local lawman, Kelly lets him take her to his apartment where she gives him a $20 taste of her "Angel Foam Champagne." Afterwards, Griff tells her she can't operate in his town, and directs her to Candy's À La Carte in the "wide open" county across the river. But Kelly decides to get away from her old line of work, and takes a job as a nurse's aid at a hospital for crippled children. She is a great success with the children and comes to the attention of Grant, the town's popular philanthropist. When they grow close, Kelly decides to tell him about her hooker past. Grant is accepting and asks her to marry him, sealing his proposal with a kiss that Kelly finds momentarily disturbing—it reminds her of a "naked kiss," the kiss of a pervert. Kelly's happiness is short-lived. She returns to Grant's house and finds him molesting a child. The young girl runs away and Kelly beats Grant to death with a telephone. When she is thrown in jail for murder, her past is exposed and the town reviles her. But she manages to find the molested little girl—conveniently playing jump-rope outside the jail cell—and all charges are dropped. The town changes its mind about Kelly, but she has had enough of their hypocrisy and takes the next bus out of town.

Constance Towers, the shaven-headed prostitute, in the brutal opening scene from *The Naked Kiss* (1964).

The Naked Kiss is a corrosive attack on bourgeois mores and double standards. Kelly is a typical Fuller outsider, living beyond the law but adhering to her own firm code of ethics. Only as a spy can she enter "polite" society. The film's central irony is an indictment of those who would judge and condemn by appearances: a prostitute becomes Grantville's savior while Mr. Grant, its leading citizen, is a deviate, a child molester.

But beneath the story's anti-moralist moral lies a web of more ambivalent examples of deceptive appearances. Everywhere in *The Naked Kiss* are masks, false fronts and self-delusions. Kelly's teased-hair wig hides a naked scalp and her pimp's humiliating punishment. As the new hooker in Grantville, she claims to be peddling champagne ("goes down like liquid gold") while Candy's whorehouse pretends to offer only "bon bons." The crippled children see themselves running in the park ("I have legs! I have legs!" one boy cries) and a romantic reverie with Grant transports Kelly to a gondola in Venice (Fuller home movie footage again!). Kelly deludes herself into believing that Grant wants to marry her in spite of her previous career as a prostitute, but he has actually chosen her *because* of her outlaw past, thinking she will be his partner in vice. ("Our marriage will be a paradise," he says just before she clobbers him with a phone.) "Your reference is your face," the

sweet old landlady tells her, but in fact every character sees something different in Kelly's face, and Kelly herself decides to give up prostitution after staring into a mirror and not recognizing what she sees.

Unbearable and fascinating, *The Naked Kiss,* along with *Shock Corridor,*
shows Fuller severing the last ties to Hollywood standards of genre and good
taste, creating harsh, wholly original story forms to contain his unconventional interests and nihilistic vision. With censorship and stylistic restraints
disappearing, the 1960s should have been the perfect decade for Fuller's explosive imagination and formal experiments. Unfortunately, *Shock Corridor*
and *The Naked Kiss* would be both the beginning and the end of an intriguing
phase in Fuller's career.

After long sojourns in Europe, and projects falling through for various
reasons, Fuller did not make another film until 1967. *Shark,* a Mexican production, was a disaster. Based on an obscure novel by Victor Canning, the
film is an adventure story set in the Sudan. Caine, played by Burt Reynolds,
is an out-of-work gun runner who hooks up with a mysterious couple, Anna
and Professor Mallare. Their greedy search for a sunken treasure leads to
assorted double and triple crosses and in the end only Caine is left alive.
Fuller disowns the picture, saying that it was taken away from him and recut,
but it is hard to imagine how much he could have improved it. The production is poor, the photography atrocious. Trivial conversations go on to the
point of unbearable tedium. Some good underwater scenes are so poorly integrated that they have the effect of stock footage. Only Arthur Kennedy's
performance as a drunken doctor brings a few moments of life to this torpid
movie. It remained unreleased for nearly three years after filming, getting a
limited distribution in 1969.

Dead Pigeon on Beethoven Street (1972) is another disappointment, a
misconceived effort that veers between incoherence and self-parody. Financed
and filmed in West Germany, this mostly light-hearted detective/interna-
tional intrigue tale concerns the efforts of an American private eye, Sandy,
to retrieve some incriminating film of his client, a U.S. senator, from a team
of blackmailers. Linking up with the criminals, Christa, a seductive blonde
(played by Christa Lang, Fuller's wife), and Mensur, Sandy participates in the
blackmailing of assorted political figures, hoping he can eventually get his
hands on Mensur's files. Sandy falls for Christa and they plan to go away
together as soon as he can get the file on the senator. After a swordfight of
sorts in Mensur's inner sanctum, Sandy kills him and grabs the film. He
doesn't count on Christa showing up for a last-minute double cross. She
shoots him, but Sandy manages to get away. Lying on the ground on Beethoven Street, Sandy has one last confrontation with Christa. She is about
to finish him off, but Sandy kills her first.

After the humorously self-reflexive opening credits, showing cast and
crew in carnival costumes and staring into the camera, *Dead Pigeon* erupts

with a display of cinematic razzle-dazzle, a flurry of images, a complex montage, a nonsensically complicated tough-guy narration. The film's first reels seem for all the world like Fuller attempting to ape his most notable admirer, Godard, imitating the highbrow playfulness of *Bande a Part* or *Alphaville*. These early scenes, with their New Wave self-indulgence, are lightly entertaining. The fun dissipates as Fuller begins to tell his story straight. A confused script is further hobbled by an abundance of amateurish German actors and third rate photography and sound. The film's nadir is reached in the incredible, ill-conceived brawl between private eye Glenn Corbett and arch villain Anton Diffring, an embarrassing sword-spear-battleaxe–slinging torrent that seems like something out of a Tex Avery cartoon.

Dead Pigeon received scant distribution, and Fuller would not make another film for eight years.

The Big Red One (1980) should have been Fuller's magnum opus. He carried the story of his combat experiences around in his head and in various stages of development for over three decades, and the film's combination of sweeping history and undisguised autobiography makes it the logical climax to a career always closely associated with the war genre. Indeed, Fuller's "comeback" garnered the kind of sympathy and respectful attention from the mainstream press usually reserved for "lifetime achievement" award winners. From the evidence of individual scenes and the novelized version of the story, it is obvious that Fuller was fully capable of creating a masterpiece, an epic yet highly personal telling of the century's biggest yarn of all. *The Big Red One* is a film full of brilliant scenes and is skillfully and imaginatively made throughout, but it is held back from its potential greatness by a niggardly budget and the tinkering of too many post-production hands.

The film is the story of the First Infantry Division—known from their armpatch as The Big Red One—as seen through the eyes of four young soldiers and their veteran sergeant. Fuller eliminates all grand perspectives and overall goals of the war, concentrating solely on the day-by-day, battle-by-battle viewpoint of his handful of GIs as they move from North Africa to Sicily to the D-Day invasion of Normandy and on to Czechoslovakia and the last fighting of the war. His intimate knowledge of World War II combat is evidenced in the film's nuts-and-bolts detailing—the condoms on the rifle bores, the dressing of wounds, the construction of the "Bangalore Relay," and assorted other exotic and trivial bits of business that foot soldier Fuller had stored in his memory bank. But *Big Red One* is no documentary. Fuller invests many scenes with a dark lyricism—the black-and-white prologue with the mad horse, the passage of time on Omaha Beach told by the wristwatch on an arm floating in a sea of blood, the haunting image of Lee Marvin's Sergeant walking with a dead child on his shoulders. Elsewhere Fuller's flamboyant inventiveness with scenes is well displayed, notably in the sequence

A village girl presents the Sergeant (Lee Marvin) with a helmet adorned with flowers in *The Big Red One* (1980).

at the French insane asylum and the closing shot of a crazed inmate firing a machine gun at all and sundry, screaming, "I am one of you—I am sane!"

The budgetary restrictions of what was, ironically, the most expensive production of Fuller's career to date are woefully apparent at times. The D-Day invasion is staged with such skimpy materiel and manpower that it appears to be less an invasion than a commando raid. Scenes that are supposedly taking place in Northern and Eastern Europe have the same khaki, sunbaked Mediterranean look of the North African and Sicilian sequences (the movie was shot almost entirely in Israel). At times the cost-cutting results in strained abstraction ("The whole German Army was on the run," says the narrator, while the screen shows a single, silhouetted German running into the horizon). But Fuller, ever inventive with a tight budget, does manage to take conceptual advantage of the production restrictions, making this a history in closeup, artfully restricted to the tunnel vision of five infantrymen.

Ultimately, the most destructive blow to the film was not the production budget but the post-production turmoil. Studio interference at the editing stage reportedly eliminated much combat violence, adding overly literal narration to self-explanatory imagery, and forcing the film's running time down from a four-hour director's cut to 113 minutes, a paltry length for a film of this scope. *The Big Red One* is a distinguished and highly entertaining motion picture, but not the masterwork it might have been. Perhaps, in the tradition of other similarly truncated films, *The Big Red One* may one day be restored to something closer to the director's original version.

White Dog (1982), an adaptation of a fact-based novella by Romain Gary, had been in development at Paramount for several years, with half a dozen screenwriters and directors involved (including Roman Polanski and Arthur Penn) before Fuller was offered the project. The film's producer, Jon Davidson, has said that Fuller was hired because he was the only man in Hollywood who could "rewrite a script and be ready to shoot it in ten days," but this is short-sighted. It would be difficult to imagine a more appropriate matchup of subject matter and sensibility. Like *Shock Corridor*, *White Dog* is a metaphoric horror story, another nightmarish tale of American madness.

The film opens on a pitch black road in a Los Angeles canyon. In the darkness a car runs into a stray dog. The driver, young actress Julie Sawyer, rushes the dog to an animal hospital and then takes it home, hoping to find its owner. One night a man breaks into Julie's house and attacks her and the dog responds with a violent assault on the intruder. When Julie brings the dog to the movie studio where she is working, it attacks and seriously injures a black actress. Shaken, Julie takes the dog to an animal training camp run by two men, Carruthers and Keys. Julie learns that her German shepherd is a "white dog," one that has been conditioned to attack and kill black people on sight. Keys, a black man, feels challenged to "deprogram" the dog, and begins a series of brutal encounters with the animal. Caged at night, the dog still manages to escape, and makes vicious attacks on other blacks. Keys finds the dog and knows what it has done, but he is obsessed with the idea of reconditioning it and so refuses to kill the animal or report it to the police. Meanwhile, Julie encounters the white dog's original owner and trainer. It turns out to be a benign-looking old man, accompanied by his two innocent young granddaughters. Revulsed by what he has done to the dog, Julie curses the man and refuses to return his "pet." At the camp, Keys believes he has finally

One of the talented canines playing the title role in *White Dog* (1982).

succeeded in "curing" the dog of its violent racism, but the strain on the dog's psyche has been too much. Its killer instincts are now triggered by the arrival of a white man—Keys' partner. To save Carruthers' life, Keys regretfully shoots and kills the animal.

The press surrounding *The Big Red One* tended to position Fuller as a nostalgia item—an "old pro" working in an out-of-date genre, making a film that, as one critic wrote, "revels in its own old-fashioned movieness." If it had been released, *White Dog* would have stopped any further critical condescension. Its icy tone and smooth, Steadicam-driven imagery could have been the work of any film-school-grad Hollywood wunderkind, and its genre—the *Jaws*–inspired real-life monster movie—was strictly *au courant*. Of course, Fuller has much more in mind than the canine equivalent of another glossy shark or slasher thrill machine. *White Dog* is an anti-racist fable, a distinctly Fullerian examination of bigotry and the dark soul of America. As in *The Crimson Kimono*, racism can appear in the least likely places. As in *The Naked Kiss*, ugly violence is hidden beneath a surface of normalcy and respectability—here a loyal German shepherd and a jolly grandpa. As in *Shock Corridor*, hatred and racism lead inevitably to madness. "You're going to see a dog slowly go insane and then come back to sanity in front of you," is how Fuller described the film's dramatic essence.

White Dog is an imaginatively conceived, boldly told and harrowingly intense attack on the psychotic nature of racism, with a strong and complex black hero in Paul Winfield's obsessed animal trainer, Keys. Yet, in an ironic eventuality that only a master of paradox like Fuller himself could properly appreciate, the film was loudly denounced as racist by a handful of black "spokespersons." Less flagrantly absurd complaints concerned fears that the subject matter would incite violence or that racists would be inspired to obtain their own white dogs. Executives at Paramount quickly decided that the film's profit potential was not worth the risks of an ugly controversy and they scrapped all plans to give *White Dog* a U.S. theatrical release. It was released in Europe, to mostly rave reviews. The NBC television network offered to buy the film and then withdrew the offer. *White Dog* was eventually shown on a minor cable television network. It did not have its official U.S. premiere until 1991, 10 years after its completion.

Fuller's next film, *Les Voleurs de la Nuit* (*Thieves After Dark*; 1982), was a French production, with entirely Gallic subject matter. The story concerns a young couple who meet in an unemployment office. François (played by Bobby Di Cicco from *The Big Red One*) is an out-of-work musician; Isabelle is an unemployed art historian. The couple get into a brawl with some arrogant bureaucrats and they leave the unemployment office in a hurry. François and Isabelle decide to team up and try making a living as street musicians. This doesn't work out and Isabelle comes up with a plan to rob the arrogant civil servants from the unemployment office. While they are in the process of burglarizing one of the bureaucrats he falls out of a window. Isabelle believes she is responsible for the man's death, and the homicide detectives agree with her. François and Isabelle go on the run, managing to elude their pursuers until the film's fateful and tragic climax.

With subject matter and setting that might have been more appropriate for a young Truffaut, Fuller's work on *Les Voleurs* is far from his best. The pace is lethargic for the first half of the film, and the handling of scenes and actors is often awkward. The film picks up as it goes along, however, and becomes quite involving by the end. Despite a good deal of stilted dialogue, Veronique Jannot and Di Cicco make a sympathetic and attractive pair of young lovers. *Les Voleurs* was not well received in France, where the local critical consensus was that Fuller had gotten out of his depth in making such an idiosyncratically French story. At any rate, the film was not a financial success and it has never been shown theatrically in America.

Fuller's last film to date is *Street of No Return* (1989), a French production shot on location in Lisbon, Portugal. *Street* is adapted from the novel of the same name by David Goodis, the depressive American master of bleak crime paperbacks and story source for the films *Dark Passage, Shoot the Piano Player* and *The Moon in the Gutter*. It was an inspired pairing of talents by

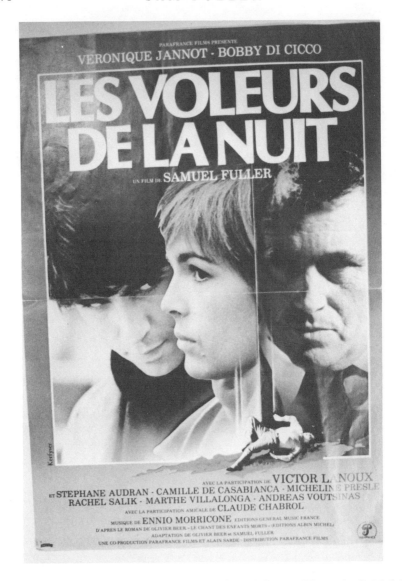

Poster for Fuller's French production, *Les Voleurs de la Nuit (Thieves in the Night)*.

producer (and co-scripter) Jacques Bral. While faithful to the dark spirit of the original, Fuller invests every frame of the film version with his own inflamed passion and outrageous, eccentric personality. He takes Goodis' Skid Row sonnet and turns it into a delirious *noir* extravaganza. From the startling opening shot of a hammer puncturing a man's face to the dreamlike happy ending, Fuller gathers up all the ingredients of a near-lifetime of mean streets storytelling and boils them down to their essence. As *The Big Red One* was to his war movies, so is *Street of No Return* the culmination of Fuller's work in the crime genre, a creative summation of all those past tales of violence and revenge and *l'amour fou*.

On downtown streets ravaged by a spectacular race riot, a haunted-looking derelict (Keith Carradine) runs into a face from his past. Bertha, a zaftig, tough-talking moll, doesn't recognize him ("Blow, bum!" she snarls), but Carradine follows her to her destination and finds there a houseful of familiar faces — Eddie, the film's slick entrepreneur-villain, and Celia, its fateful Circe. The derelict's memory is stirred, and a long flashback takes him to the time when he was Michael, a rich and famous rock musician. Michael sees Celia performing a sexy stage act and has to meet her. They have an intensely erotic affair and Michael wants her to run away with him. Celia is afraid of leaving her vicious boyfriend, Eddie, but finally agrees to meet Michael at the train station. Only Eddie shows up. Later, Eddie and his gang, with Celia in tow, decide to teach Michael a lesson, cutting the rock singer's throat and destroying his career. The flashback over, Michael the derelict (who speaks only in a strained whisper) wanders back to the debris-strewn city, sucking alcoholic sustenance from the jagged bottom of a broken liquor bottle. He is sitting beside the body of a dead policeman when some other cops arrive, blame him for the murder, and sweep him off to the police station where Borel, the police captain (played with wild-eyed charisma by Bill Duke), is berating a roomful of arrested rioters. Using a powerful water hose, Michael is able to start a riot of his own and escapes from the station. He befriends the owner of a junkyard, who recognizes him from his past identity and shows him an old music video that features Celia as a bare-breasted enchantress. Michael is taken hostage by a group of rioter-revolutionaries headquartered on an old freighter. Escaping, he hitches a car ride that fatefully takes him back to Eddie and Celia's villa. He breaks in and overhears a conversation between Eddie and the leader of the revolutionaries. It seems that Eddie has been engineering the street riots as part of a real estate scam to bring down property values. Michael goes back to Borel and tells him of Eddie's plans, which include getting rid of Borel. The police raid the house and most of Eddie's gang is killed. With Borel's permission, Michael has his revenge: aiming a pistol at Eddie's testicles, Michael tells him, "Now I'm just gonna change *your* voice a little," and shoots. Michael returns to Skid Row but Celia comes for him. Together they walk off into the night.

By any standard, *Street of No Return* is a wildly entertaining movie. One can sense Fuller having a ball with the material on screen — the kitschy music video, the bloody riot staged like a Rio *carnaval*, the over-the-top, B-movie tough-guyisms of Bill Duke's Borel and Rebecca Potok's cigar-smoking Bertha (only the second time Fuller has been able to stick one of his female characters with a stogie). His visual creativity is generously displayed. The

Keith Carradine amid the post-riot rubble in *Street of No Return,* adapted from a
novel by David Goodis.

seedy desperation of the alcoholic is evoked in a single overhead shot of
Michael groveling beneath a liquor bottle overturned on a high shelf, catching the falling drops on his tongue. Fuller matches past feats of intricate *mise-
en-scène* — Eddie and gang dumping Michael and driving away, filmed in one
take from the car hood with a slow zoom out, dazzlingly composed with three
planes of action and a moving vehicle. *Street's* haunting but unstudied images reinvent the photographic iconography of *film noir* with the blue and
red fluorescent glow of a modern urban midnight. Dreamy and at times
outright illogical, Fuller's film seems to come directly from the ravaged
memory of its hero. Plot points and transitions are painted with broad
strokes, and the port town setting is a ghostly Esperantoville (a Third World-
ish America somewhere in Europe), in effect a hallucinatory nowhere. But
Fuller has seldom been concerned with the incidentals of surface realism or
naturalistic behavior. *Street* exists in the self-contained alternate universe of
the filmmaker — grotesque, absurd, lyrical, sublime.

Working with Fuller

The following commentaries are adapted from interviews I have conducted with a cross-section of Sam Fuller's creative collaborators.

Vincent Price

Actor: *Baron of Arizona*

We made *Baron of Arizona* in eighteen or twenty days, something like that. And it was a lot of work, awfully hard to do in that time. But the people in it, Beulah Bondi and Ellen Drew and Vladimir Sokoloff, were all so professional that we could get on with it and get it done. I had done some fast pictures at Fox under my contract, and one very good one called *Shock*. We did them in nineteen or twenty days and I found that you could do it. And it's really much more fun to do because it's like doing a play, you can have a real feeling for the material. I always found that the films I liked most were the ones where we got on and did it and didn't waste time. I mean, *The Song of Bernadette* took nine months to shoot and by the time you got through you forgot what the name of your character was.

I never did know how Sammy got James Wong Howe to photograph it, because Jimmy Howe I don't think had ever done a film in his life that wasn't a super high-budget film with a long shooting schedule. I was a great fan of Jimmy's before I worked with him and even more so afterwards. And *Baron of Arizona* is a beautiful looking picture. I don't understand these expensive films today—I never see the $32 million or $55 million on the screen. But Jimmy and Sammy got every penny they had up on the screen.

I didn't know of Sammy before we worked together. This was one of his first pictures and nobody had talked about him because they hadn't worked with him. But he was an excellent director and we had a very good time on the film. Sammy was a colorful character. It was a time in Hollywood when there were lots of colorful characters, and he was just a little more so than most of them. He saw himself as a director, and really almost a caricature of a director, with everything but the puttees and the megaphone. But he was very, very good and I never give a shit what they wear as long as they get on with it and know what they're doing.

Sammy didn't have the budget for rehearsals and you weren't allowed [by the Guild] to rehearse unless you were paid. But Sammy, like Roger Corman, was very clever, and they'd say, "Would you like to see the set?" And you'd go down and see the set and before you knew it you were walking around, getting familiar with the sets and running your lines—but I'm sure it wasn't scheduled.

The character I played was a real person, and of course the script, the ending particularly, wasn't exactly what happened. The real baron ended up as a bum on the streets of Phoenix. What we had in the film was a sort of semi-happy ending. Lippert, I think, thought it would sell at the box office better without him becoming a bum at the end. You know, Bob Lippert sold it immediately to television, which was at that point in its infancy. And I have been told that it had played more times on television at that time than any other film. And it got a reaction from a lot of people because it was on the new medium and everybody saw it a dozen times. I think Lippert made back his money right away on *Baron of Arizona*.

I really enjoyed making the film and I am very proud of it. I liked Sammy a lot—he was flamboyant but he was good. We became friendly during the shoot and we saw each other socially. I liked Sammy and I liked his wife. But then we all went off to do other things, make other pictures. As you look back on as long a career as I've had, what is so very unsettling about making movies is that you become friendly and close with people during the shoot and then you go your separate ways, and you don't stay in touch or even keep up with their careers. And, really, you end up a long career with very few intimate friends from all those years of working with people.

Gene Evans

Actor: *The Steel Helmet, Fixed Bayonets, Park Row, Hell and High Water, Shock Corridor*

The day I met Sam, I was mad, really pissed off. I had been all day traveling around to the studios. I didn't know anything about Hollywood, and I had a six-foot-six-inch Swede agent, and I was this big redheaded . . . we were a very strange team. Anyway, I had been to two other interviews and things hadn't gone well and I was tired and pissed off. And this was an open cattle-call and a lot of people had already been to this thing. And I went in, and he never said to sit down or anything. He was behind a desk, with the cigar in his mouth, and he starts rattling questions at me. "Were you in the army?" That was the first thing he said, with the cigar in his mouth. I said, "Yeah." He said, "Were you in the infantry?" I said, "No, I wasn't in the infantry." And he said, "Then you weren't in the army." I said, "I was in the combat engineers, and we cleaned up everything you guys couldn't." And he says, "Huh, is that a fact?" I said, "Yeah." He said, "Where were you on D-Day?" I said, "On D-plus-2 I was on the beach." He said, "Is that a fact?" And all this time he's got an M1 laying across his desk. And I had been overseas for three years, but I still remembered the horror of basic training, when those little lieutenants would come up and snatch your rifle out of your hands, look it over, and when you least expect it *jam* it back at you. And I'm watching this guy behind the desk pretty close because he looked pretty sneaky to me. All of a sudden, boy, he shot that thing at me—and if I hadn't been watching I believe he'd have knocked me right down with it because he really shot it at me. And I caught it. He said, "Rack it back." I didn't think, I just threw my hands down and worked the receiver. I got the thumb out, which was the trick. And then I pitched it back to him. He put the rifle down on the table and asks me to read him a line of dialogue. I read it. Then he says, "Come on, let's go upstairs. I want you to talk to somebody." And we went upstairs to somebody's office and he says, "I found my Zack."

We went to see the associate producer, a little dress manufacturer named Murray Lerner. I didn't know what the hell was going on. The agent made the deal—I got a thousand dollars for the picture. It was going to take ten days to shoot. It was all very, very strange to me. And Sammy did ask me what my name was, eventually.

My part wasn't all that big in the beginning. Bob Hutton was the lead in the picture originally, with the top billing. About the second day of shooting he cut his hand in an explosion—Sammy was always big for explosions on the set, I'll say that for him. So he set off this helluva explosion and everybody's supposed to hit the deck, and Bob Hutton got a sliver up his finger or something—he started wailing. So he couldn't work right away. And Fuller said to me, "How fast can you learn dialogue?" I said, "Pretty fast." I had a hunch my part was about to get bigger. I said, "Pretty damn fast." So from then on my part started changing a lot, and my part got a lot heavier. Sammy would sit down at the typewriter and come back with some pretty yellow paper and tell you you had fifteen minutes to learn the new lines. And I could do it. I had worked in the theater, and I'd had a scholarship in the Pasadena Playhouse before I went in the army. I knew what I was doing. I was a good actor and I knew I was good, no problems with confidence. And that was important with Sammy because he could throw you, he could blow your mind. Sammy was a tough, tough guy to work for. But I got along fine with him. We got along great. And he stuck with me.

I think we were about four or five days into the shooting of the picture and I thought it was going swimmingly. He asked me to go to the rushes and I looked at the stuff—I could see where I could have done better with a little more time, but it looked pretty good to me. So I was happy with my part and what I was doing with it. But then on about the fourth day, Lerner came down to me on the set and called me over. He said, "Listen, this isn't really working out the way we had hoped. We're going to pay you, don't worry, but another man has become available for the part." They were going to give me the whole thousand dollars and reshoot my three days of scenes with another actor. I can remember the terrible feeling I had. I thought I had been doing well—was it possible that I had fooled myself completely? I had thought Fuller liked what I was doing, but Fuller never ran up to you and said, "That's great!" Just "Print it!" So Lerner told me this and I didn't know what to say. I said, "Well, I want to do the picture, but if that's what you want to do..."

I went back to the set. They were working again. Sammy says, "Cut! What the hell's the matter?" I told him how I felt about it. He said, "What the hell are you talking about?" I told him. Wow! He blew up! He said, "You stay right here." And he went up to their offices above the sound stage. He went up and he came right down. He found out what was going on. This was right at the time of the Un-American hearings and McCarthy and all that stuff, and Larry Parks had just testified against a lot of people and got cleared. And Murray Lerner had a brainstorm: Larry Parks was unemployed, they could afford him, and at that moment everybody in the country was hearing about Larry Parks—what a coup it would be, Murray Lerner decided, if they hired Larry Parks for my part in the picture.

Fuller just went absolutely crazy. He came boiling back down to the sound stage. He said, "Get your script. Let's get the hell out of here! This place is history!" So we went out and got into his car. He said, "You're living in the fleabag hotel across the street?" And I was. He says, "Go in and get your suitcase." And I went but I came back. I said, "I owe them two hundred dollars." Well, he gave me the money. I went in, got my suitcase and got in the car with him—I didn't have a car. I had been working for four or five years but I wasn't exactly killin' 'em. There wasn't a lot of money. So I went with him up to his house and we stayed there—I stayed there for the rest of the picture, in fact. And all day we were there and there were threats, calls from my agent. And that night they finally backed down and we went back and finished the picture. And from then on there was a sign hanging, as big as the stage door: "No producers—producers, co-producers, executive producers—no one admitted."

It was a hard picture to do. They had no money. We shot all the exteriors in Griffith Park. The big scene where I was blown up we didn't shoot till much later—where I raise up after the big explosion and say, "Where is everybody?" We shot that with no crew, no money, no permit. I forget where the hell we were. They shot it with a hand-held camera. But Sam was going to get it done one way or the other. He had tremendous enthusiasm. I liked Sam and I still like him. And I knew that the picture was going to be controversial. I knew what Sam was doing because I had been a soldier. But this was the time of McCarthy and the mood of the country was so far to the right. I was deaf on McCarthy and all that stuff, and so was Sam. But there was a lot of sentiment — just as there is again now — that if you don't grab the flag and run out in the street and start waving it and play the drum and bugle then you are not a patriot and you don't love your country. That's a lot of bullshit. So we took a lot of heat for that picture — Sammy took it, mostly. And the FBI had come to me, a guy came and questioned me about people in Hollywood that I knew. Hell, I didn't know anything about that. I wasn't a communist for chrissake. I was an actor. But they were looking for a furthering of some conspiracy. It was ridiculous. I had a Purple Heart, a Bronze Star. I had certainly served my country. And they almost made a big mistake if they had called in Sam. Sam had been all shot up in the war. If they had called him — I wish they had, I could see what they'd get — he would have taken his tie off, taken his shirt off and shown them something about fighting for your country — "Take a look at this! What have *you* given to your country?" I can't think of anybody who was more patriotic than Sam.

Steel Helmet was a big, big success, and we went to Fox for the next one, *Fixed Bayonets*. This was under contract, twenty-five hundred dollars a week. My God, there wasn't that much money in the world!

Fixed Bayonets was a hard picture. And he knew it was going to be hard. Sam decided he was going to get me in shape. He had a gal living at his house, a big black gal — kind of a cook and general factotum. And she was going with a guy called Turkey Thompson, an ex-heavyweight prizefighter. He once fought Joe Louis. And Fuller hired him and said, "I want you to get Evans in shape." I was a pretty good boozer. I mean, I loved to play every night, every night. I always did my work, but I died some days.

So one morning I'm in bed in my apartment and there's a bang on the door. I couldn't believe it. It was four-thirty or five o'clock in the morning, and I'd been to bed for about an hour. And I look out through the door and, my God, there's the biggest, meanest-looking bastard I ever saw in my life. And he's banging and I wouldn't open the door. Finally he says, "Sam Fuller sent me." I thought, "Oh boy . . ." So I let him in and he's got these heavy sweat clothes for me, wool cap and everything. I said, "Just what is it we're going to do?" He said, "We're going to do some road work." Oh my God. And he took me out to the riding trails in Griffith Park. For two weeks. Every morning we would go out and run with the fighters.

And as it turned out this was the best thing in the world because *Fixed Bayonets* was one tough shoot and a lot of guys got hurt. It was a hell of a thing to shoot. Ice on the ground, very hard to keep your footing. And it was hot on the sound stage, my God it was hot and we were all in snow clothes, bundled up in blankets. A lot of people got hurt, and everybody had a twisted ankle trying to get around on that ice. Some of the stunt men got hurt, and they were the most able guys physically of the whole bunch. One of the stunt guys we carried on a stretcher for the whole picture, like he was wounded. And he was wounded—I think he broke his leg. And Fuller kept him on-camera, wouldn't let him off the picture.

I got into a fight with Sam at one point. He had a shot he wanted me to do—I had to come down off the mountain, go down the side of the cliff, across the ice, and up the other side which was just as steep as going down, and then into a bayonet fight on the other side with some UCLA students. He wanted it all in one take—he had a huge crane he was riding and he wanted to follow me with the camera for the whole thing. And we did it over and over. I said, "Why don't you get a stunt man?" He said, "I'm going to be right on your face in this shot." Well, he wasn't right on my face the way they shot it. But I did it again, the whole thing, on the biggest sound stage in Hollywood. About the fifth time, I couldn't get up the ladder to get back up to the cave. Somebody had to get under me and get practically between my legs to get me up there. And I was at the mouth of the cave and I could not get my breath, I was so exhausted. And Sam is sitting on the boom with the cameraman, and he says, "Come on! What's the matter, ya pussy!" And I said, "Why, you little cocksucker!" And Sam reacts. He's on the boom, fifty-five feet up—he's on a level with me, but there's eight feet of air between us. And he's so mad he starts to step off the crane, to come at me. And just as he's about to walk right off the boom the cameraman, Lucien Ballard, reaches out and catches him by the back of the belt and jerks him back onto the boom. And then when he got down we made up and laughed it off and everything. And Sam says to Lucien, "My God, Lucien, thank you for pulling me back. I would have stepped right off the boom—fifty feet up." And I don't know if you know about the mechanics of these booms but they are carefully balanced for the weight they will carry and if Sam had stepped off the thing would have gone right through the roof of the sound stage. And Lucien says, "Don't thank me, it was nothing. I didn't care what happened to you, but I was sure as hell didn't want my head shot through the sound stage!"

Then there was the day on the picture—I'll never forget this—Sam was going to shoot the retreat. He wanted to shoot a long line of soldiers retreating, and they put out a call for around two hundred extras. And it was a bad day because there were a lot of action pictures shooting, and all the usual extras were working. They couldn't get enough of them. But there was a big musical just finished shooting and the guy who got the extras rounded up all these chorus boys and dancers from the musicals. And they went to wardrobe and got their helmets and uniforms and rifles and they came on the set. Fuller arrives and he starts looking them over and he sees some things that don't look right on his soldiers. One of these extras has his collar turned up in a kind of stylish way. And another one's got his cuffs all nicely turned back. And Sam stops and says, "What, what is that? Why do you have those cuffs turned back?" And the extra says to him, "Well, I want to *look nice!*"

Sam knew there was something a little different but he didn't know what it was. The extras would be marching around and he'd say, "Look at the way that guy's moving! He's supposed to be a soldier retreating! What is this?" So finally I said, "Sam, those guys are dancers — they're gay." And Sam knows a few things very well — mainly motion pictures — but to a whole lot of things he's oblivious. And he says, "*Dancers? Gay?*" And he just chomps that cigar in his mouth and studies them. Finally, he figures out what he's got to do. He had some crafts people bring out some big lead weights, fifty-pound weights, and he had these extras wear the fifty-pound weights and he had them marching around the set, back and forth until they were complaining and cursing and some of them were hiding. And by God, after that they really looked like a bunch of tired, retreating soldiers. And Sam gave them a speech, through the loudspeaker. He's got the cigar and he says, "Now you guys are dead tired, and you're defeated soldiers, and you're retreating to the rear." But hell, these dancers didn't do war movies and they didn't know one end of the weapons from the other end. And I was standing there listening to Fuller when a guy next to me let out the damndest scream you ever heard. He had a rifle, an M1 with the bayonet fixed, and he's got the rifle butt-end up, he's bored, and he's resting his chin on the butt, resting the bayonet on his boot, and he drove the bayonet right through and into his foot. Fuller couldn't believe it. But he kept him on, made a casualty out of him so he could get a paycheck.

After that we did *Park Row* together. He had deals to make the picture and they fell through and finally he put up his own dough, and it cost him a lot of money. He did it right, too, built a tremendous set, and opened it big at Graumann's Chinese Theatre. And the picture was a critical success, but it didn't make any money. And Sam had given me a piece of that one! But somebody said in regards to that picture, that the only thing the public cares about newspapers is whether it's on their porch in the morning.

Sam really worked himself into a lather on that picture. It was made in fourteen days or so, and with a lot of innovations. He used that crab dolly like it had never been used before. This story was the love of Sam's life and it was kind of a catharsis for him, to put all his thoughts about the newspaper business on film. His office was done up like an editor's office of an old time newspaper. And he was like a kid in a candy store when all those newspaper mastheads from across the United States came in, to be put on the crawl behind the titles. And that was really something.

Sam liked to shoot long takes, and you would have to learn sometimes ten pages of dialogue. He would lay out these long scenes, and move the camera around and move in and move back and all around you, and just go on shooting until he ran out of film. And he would have fight scenes in there that he wanted you to do in one take, beginning to end. And there was one long sequence with a fight in it, and Sam is describing what to do and he says, "And then you roll underneath the wagon and fight over to the other side." I said, "What wagon?" He says, "The wagon that's going to be coming down the street." I said, "The wagon's going to be moving down the street?" I said, "You're crazy!" That Sammy, you had to be careful with him or you could get hurt.

That was the hardest picture I ever did. I went from two hundred twenty pounds to about one seventy-five during that picture. The tight clothes and everything, and we worked hard and fast. I was just drained. And still I tried to play all night, every night. I look back and I don't know what the hell kept me from dying.

Then Sam did *Pickup on South Street* and I'd have killed to be in it. I wanted to do the part that Mervyn Vye did. Man, I wanted to do it. But I was making a picture with Tony Quinn, a terrible movie from a Mickey Spillane book, *The Long Wait*. But then we did *Hell and High Water* together at Fox, with Widmark. And we were about to get started on the picture when Sammy calls me to come up to his house. And I go and he says, "I want you to do a big favor for me. I want you to help Bella Darvi with her lines." I said, "Who's Bella Darvi?" He said, "She's going to be the leading lady." I said, "I don't do that kind of work." And he says, "But you could, you'd be very good at it. And she likes you." I said, "Why is that? I don't even know her." He says, "Don't worry, she knows you, she likes you." So he had me helping her with her dialogue. And while I was helping her I had a birthday and there was a birthday party and Bella is hanging all over me, smooching me, saying how wonderful I am to be helping her at night, and there's photographers and she's kissing me for the photographers. And she gives me a birthday present, these expensive silver pieces. And I look at them and they have initials on the silver, "DFZ"—Darryl F. Zanuck. And I ask Widmark and I find out Bella Darvi is Zanuck's "discovery," she's living at his house. And I was looking to get a nice fat contract with Fox, and here's Bella Darvi kissing me for the photographers, and the silver, and I could see my career at Fox going through the window.

After *Hell and High Water* the last picture I did with Sam was *Shock Corridor*. That was a difficult character. Sam called and said, "I don't know anybody else who can do this part." He didn't have any money, but it didn't make any difference—I would have done it for nothing, anyway. It was difficult to get that character just right. It needed a hell of a transition. The guy was like a child one moment and then all of a sudden there's an about-face and he starts talking physics, the A-bomb, scientific stuff. A hell of a switch. And unless it came off just swimmingly it was going to be bad. And I had broken my finger just before I did it. I was in a fight in a joint down on

Short Round (William Chun) examines Sergeant Zack's (Gene Evans) bullet-scarred helmet. From *The Steel Helmet* (1951).

Melrose, near Paramount. I hit a guy just as hard as I could hit him, and he went down and got right up. And I went running to get out the door, because I didn't need any more of that guy. And I had a busted finger from when I hit him. I went to a clinic and they put a sling on it, but Sam said, "You can't work with that on. That looks ridiculous." So I took it off and after a couple of days I've got a bent finger. And Sam says, "Well, that's what you get for going out fooling around."

But that part in *Shock Corridor* was about the hardest acting I ever had to do. I did it once and I thought I could do it better. Sam worked fast and sometimes when I thought I could do something better he'd say, "You'll never do it better, let's go on." But on *Shock Corridor* I got him to let me try the thing over again, and the second time I really nailed it.

I always enjoyed working with Sam. Don't misunderstand, we had a lot of fights, arguments, really vehement ones. He would fight at the drop of a hat, over anything. But never anything that didn't get settled that same afternoon. And when we were making *Park Row,* and everything had to go fast, it was all money out of his pocket, he heard that my mother had come to visit the set. And he just stopped everything and introduced her to everybody.

She was from a little town in California and she brought a friend of hers, and she was so impressed with Sam, such a gentleman and courtly towards her.

A few years back they had a retrospective of Sam's work at USC. They were showing *Steel Helmet* and Sam was going to be there to answer questions afterward. Arthur Knight called me from USC and asked if I would be there as a sort of surprise guest — walk out on the stage and surprise Sam. And I said okay. I hadn't seen Sammy in ten or fifteen years at that point.

A long time ago Sam had given me the helmet from the picture, with the bullet hole in it, as a Christmas present. It was right after the picture had come out and I knew how much money he was making on the picture because his business manager was giving me the checks for him — forty and fifty thousand dollars a week. And I went to Sammy's Christmas party at his house. Darryl and Virginia Zanuck were there, and Hedda Hopper. Hedda Hopper played Santa Claus and they gave out all these lavish presents. And the last present was for me, from Sammy. And with all that money coming in from the picture I knew it had to be a solid gold something or a big stack of money. And it was the helmet. And I didn't know what to say. I was disappointed, but I was touched. Anyway, I kept that helmet with the bullet hole all this time and when I was coming down to USC from Ventura where I was living I put the helmet in a white plastic sack. And when I came out on stage and surprised Sam I was carrying that sack. And after the excitement of us being together on the stage died down, Sam says, "What have you got in that sack? Everybody in the place is looking at that damn sack and nobody's looking at my cigar!" And I said, "I've got a head in there." He says, "Come on!" And I took the steel helmet out and I said, "I've enjoyed it for all these years, and I thought it was time to give it back." He was pretty torn up. Hell, he couldn't even talk.

It has been very nice being associated with Sam. Made a big difference in my life. I've done a lot of good pictures with a lot of different people, but the ones with Sam are the ones people seem to remember. About a week or so ago, I was stopped at a red light and a black cat drove up beside me. He was looking, staring at me, and all of a sudden he snaps his fingers, smiles, and says, *"If you die, I'll kill you!"* I thought, my God, how about that . . . who'd ever think somebody'd remember a line you said in a picture, all those years ago.

Richard Widmark

Actor: *Pickup on South Street, Hell and High Water*

We always thought of Sam in those days as kind of the Grandma Moses of filmmaking. His style was very primitive, direct, journalistic. He was an

ex-newspaperman and he got right to the point of the story and the characters. I had seen *The Steel Helmet,* with Gene Evans, and that was very good,
efficient kind of fimmaking in the "B" category. Sam was very good at that
very lean, tough approach. No wasted motion, no wasted words.

He was a very colorful little guy. I remember when I first came to work
with him on *Pickup on South Street,* he had been doing all these war pictures
and he was used to starting scenes by shooting off a gun. That meant "action." And he shot this gun once on the set and I went over to him and said,
"Sam, don't ever do that again." And he didn't. No more shooting. At least
not on our picture. And that was our only "confrontation." We got along great
after that. I liked Sam a lot. He was a tough little guy and I enjoyed him very
much.

Sam and Zanuck in that period were very close. Zanuck liked his approach—as long as the pictures did well—and they were aligned intellectually.
They were very much alike in personality. I remember, Zanuck always smoked
about a foot-long cigar, and so did Sam, and Sam says, "I've got to have a bigger cigar than Zanuck," and so he got cigars that were two inches longer.

Both pictures I did with Sam were assignments. There wasn't any discus-
sion about "what was going to be our approach" or anything like that. It was
an assignment. I was under contract and in those days I was making four, five
pictures a year. I finished one on Saturday, started another on Monday. They
give you your next script and you do it or you go on suspension. I liked Sam's
script—it was a good, tight script. But I'm trying to say that we just did it.
No talk, no discussions about motivation, no baloney. Just do it. Four weeks,
all on the set, all at Fox. Even exteriors. That little house where the character
lives on the dock, just a set. No finesse, just quick, in and out, get it done.
On to the next one. So unlike today where each picture they think is a major
project and you have to go through all sorts of trauma to get it done.

We had a good cast for *Pickup on South Street.* Jean—Jean Peters—was
a terrific girl. We were both under contract at that time. She was from Ohio
State and Zanuck found her someplace. . . . I think she won a beauty contest,
and he brought her out. A real nice girl. And we did work on our scenes together. We rehearsed together in a room for about a week and we got a bead
on our characters. And we worked out how we would do any business we had
to do together. Was there a scene where I was slapping her? I was always slapping somebody in those days. Well, we rehearsed those things by ourselves.
I enjoyed working with Jean a lot. And I liked Thelma Ritter very much as
well. I knew Thelma from the radio days back in New York. I had spent about
ten years in the theater and doing radio and I knew Thelma back in those
days, and she was always a wonderful actress and a terrific lady.

There was a big fight scene in the subway. I don't remember anything
in particular about that. It was all a set in the studio so they could control
everything. They always had stuntmen for the dangerous stuff, but I was very

active and athletic in those days and I did a lot of it myself. There was another scene where I was on this barge or whatever it was and I had to swing across the water on a rope. It wasn't really dangerous if you didn't lose your grip. But we were working at night and I went to dinner and had some daiquiris at dinner. I came back to do the shot and I just barely made it across the water without falling in.

We had a terrific cameraman on the picture, Joe MacDonald. Joe was a great help to any director. As I say, no one spent a lot of time talking about scenes, or trying different ways of placing the camera. We did it fast and got out of there. I saw the picture once, in New York, forty years ago, and I haven't seen it again.

Sam and I did one more picture together, *Hell and High Water*. It was a terrible movie, a terrible script — terrible all the way down. They threw the script at Sam, they thought he could do something with it, and he rewrote it. But it was crap. We all knew it going in. In those days, when you were under contract, you knew that half the stuff was junk but you didn't have any choice in the matter. If you wanted to keep working you did it.

Hell and High Water was in the early days of Cinemascope, and they must have been more concerned with the camera than the script. The picture was one of Zanuck's big mistakes. He made it strictly to introduce Bella Darvi as a big movie star. Bella was Zanuck's invention. She was a poor Polish girl he picked up in Paris, and they renamed her. I don't know what her real name was. Darvi was for Darryl and Virginia Zanuck. Zanuck and his wife named her after themselves. Zanuck was determined to make her a big star, but she couldn't act her way out of a paper bag. The first picture he stuck her in was *Hell and High Water*.

It was apparent to everyone that she couldn't act. Zanuck never came around the set, but he was always keeping track of how his protégée was doing. He sent me a letter thanking me for being nice to her, which I wasn't, but it was his perverse way of saying, goddammit, you better be nice to her. It was a funny letter. She hadn't been too friendly to anybody on the set, and she wasn't very receptive to me, either. Then we got to a scene where I had to give her a big shove, to get her away from this tower. And I had been looking forward to shoving her for about three weeks. I get to push Bella around — terrific! And I gave her a terrible push, unfortunately, and I regret it very much. She hit her head on something on the bottom of the set and she had to go to the infirmary to get her head patched up. And for some reason, after that she couldn't have been sweeter. I think she took it to mean I was crazy about her.

I got to sort of like her, but she was a poor lost soul. Unfortunately, she's dead now. She committed suicide some time ago.

We did that entire picture in the studio, just like the other one, and it was crap, and that was that.

I didn't see Sam again for a long time. He has become a cult in his late years. People who don't know what they're talking about read a lot of things into some of these old directors. Sam was mainly concerned with slam-bang action, and he was doing a job just like everybody else. But I like Sam and we got along fine. I saw him a couple of years ago—the first time I saw him since we finished *Hell and High Water.* I went over to Paris to do some publicity on a picture and they had a gathering afterward and there was Sam. They love him there. They think he's a genius. But Sam hadn't changed any. He was still the same nice tough little guy.

Robert Stack

Actor: *House of Bamboo*

I made a movie with Sam called *House of Bamboo.* I had never worked with him before and he didn't know me from a hot rock, and I liked the fact that we met and he made up his mind, accepted me like that. We went over to Japan to shoot the movie and I've got to tell you, it was quite an experience.

I remember, for an early scene in the picture, he had me go down to this rough part of Tokyo where there were gangs and derelicts, and a few Americans living in the streets there, winos and addicts. And he had me keep a couple days' growth of beard and wear this crappy outfit and go down there, rummage around in garbage cans for a couple of days, let the people there get used to seeing me, another renegade drunk American. And then he was going to shoot the scene with a hidden camera. On the third day I go back and he's going to film me. And remember, no one knows what the hell we were doing, the citizenry didn't know about the movie. By now they've accepted me as an old American derelict. So I'm walking around, the cameras are hidden somewhere, and all of a sudden somebody yells in Japanese. And they start coming after me like they're going to kill me. Well Jesus! I realize these guys didn't know I was an actor! I started running. They chased me down this long, long alleyway. I didn't know what I was going to do if they caught me. And finally a policeman caught up with us and is screaming in Japanese, something like "This is an actor! This is an actor! Let him go!" And that was all because Sam wanted to get some shots that looked natural. He got his way! And my wife said to me after we got out of there, "My God, I don't know if we have enough insurance for this picture!"

Sam had been a combat soldier so nothing much scared him, and he was very much into the reality of scenes. I remember one sequence we had where the gang is running away after a robbery. One of the actors was supposed to run past a half-dozen fifty-gallon oil drums. And Sam told the actor, "Now

Fuller about to signal the start of a take by firing a pistol.

look, when you pass that last fifty-gallon drum I want you to go down really *low*." Sam didn't tell him that he had a guy with a big Remington up on a parallel and he shot right over the guy's head, right into this fifty-gallon drum—blew it all to hell. "Okay, cut!" Sam says. And the actor looked up at the guy on the parallel with a gun and he damn near fainted, almost got sick to his stomach. "Jesus Christ!" he's gasping, "those were real bullets!" And Sam just said, "Don't worry, he knew what he was doing."

To Sam that was just fun and games. He loved to put people on and have some fun. He liked to keep a gun strapped to his hip while we were shooting in Japan—he looked like General Patton. And instead of saying "Action!" to start a scene, he would take a .45 out of the holster and shoot it in the air—*Boom!* And people all around would run and scurry and hide. Sam always kept things jumping. Sam and Zanuck would do things together—they were equally crazy. One time they were in a projection room at Fox. It was an underground screening room, solid cement. And Sam and Darryl are down there and Sam is carrying a German Luger. And Darryl said to him, "What is that?" "That's a Luger. A nine millimeter." "Yeah? Does it still work?" "Of course it works." "Yeah," Zanuck says, "Let's see." And Sam shot the damned nine millimeter right in the screening room and the bullet went ricocheting around off the walls—*bing, bang, bang!*

Except for one or two shots we did back at the Fox studio, all of *House of Bamboo* was filmed in Japan. This was the first big American production done there and they were not always equipped for everything Sam wanted to do. But Sam was always determined he would get the shot he had in his head and nothing was going to stop him. We did a scene around the Kamakura Buddha. Now everybody who ever shoots the Kamakura Buddha shoots *up*, tilts the camera up from the ground to show how the damn thing is way the hell up in the sky. Sam didn't want that. He wanted the camera up in the air, shooting *over* and past the Buddha and seeing the two characters walking towards it. Now we had a big Cinemascope camera, and there was no crane, no equipment in Japan to approximate what we had in the States, nothing that could go anywhere near as high as Sam wanted. So they had to rig something from scratch—they made it out of shards of bamboo and thongs, straight up into the air, and held it down with rocks. It was really primitive. And the poor camera operator with the Cinemascope camera had to go up there, floating around in the sky at the top of this thing. I still don't believe it, that poor bastard weaving around on top of this thing made of bamboo, for God's sake. But Sam got the shot he wanted. And it was quite a shot.*

It's tough when you go on location. You have to improvise, use things that weren't designed for your purposes. We shot the chase at the end at this

---

*The wooden platform can be glimpsed during James Best's home-movie "hallucination" in Shock Corridor.

semi–amusement park in Tokyo. Everything is so crowded in Tokyo that they don't have room for a Disneyland, so this amusement park is on the roof of a building. And I was supposed to chase Robert Ryan onto this rotating whirligig that hung out over the edge of this damned building, which was about thirty stories above the ground. The whirligig just barely worked — it hadn't been oiled in I don't know how long. And now they put the Cinemascope camera in there — and you must remember that the Cinemascope camera was a big, big mother — and that just completely unbalanced the whole thing. And the operator has to sit behind it, hung out there thirty stories above the ground on the side of the building. And then the actors had to go out and run around this thing. There were definitely elements of risk connected with Sam. But nobody paid any attention to it. You got swept up in Sam's attitude — you know, hellbent for leather and damn the torpedoes!

Actually, the most uncomfortable scene to shoot was one of the love scenes! It was the last sequence and I'm supposed to be getting romantic with Shirley Yamaguchi in this park surrounded by cherry trees. But it was freezing in Japan. I'm there in a shirt and Shirley's in a light dress and all the crew had their quilted jackets on. My teeth are chattering, my fingers are turning bluc and I'm supposed to be making love to Shirley Yamaguchi, and everybody in the crew is dressed like they were in the Arctic Circle. And Sam says, "Roll 'em . . . Goddamn it, warm up to her." I say, "Sonofabitch, I'm freezin'!" And there was an assistant art director up in the trees, *gluing* paper cherry blossoms to the friggin' cherry trees because those trees hadn't seen a real cherry blossom in six months!

The weather in Japan was overcast the whole time we were there. I could hardly see a shadow and I wondered how it was going to work out, but our cameraman, Joe MacDonald, adored all that haze. He said to me, "Wait till you see it on film. It'll be a postcard." And by God, it was, the photography was fabulous.

This was a tough show to do. It was not long after the war, we were the occupiers, and it was not always the most pleasant place to be. There was no big love from a lot of the young people when we were there. And there was some trouble when we went to do some stuff on the railway cars, and the workers went on strike. But in general I didn't look into the logistical problems too much because I had enough problems . . . staying alive!

It was, as I say, quite an experience. Sam fits anybody's concept of the rugged individualist. He's a throwback to the old days, those Hemingway characters, the kind of madmen the industry had for a time — Sam and Wild Bill Wellman and Budd Boetticher. Those guys made moviemaking a happening, an adventure. Sam was a writer and a student of human nature and he knew how to cut right to the heart of any scene. I'm beginning to sound like his agent. But I love Sam. How could you not like him, with that cigar, and he gets all emotional, two inches from your face, shouting, waving that cigar till you say, "Jesus, get that cigar out of my face!" But Sam is a terrific moviemaker, and he had what I find lacking in a lot of the stuff today — enthusiasm, drive, *go!*

Joseph Biroc

Director of Photography: *Run of the Arrow, China Gate, Forty Guns, Verboten*

When you work with a guy like Sam you have differences of opinion all along, because some of his ideas were so damned *crazy!* But Sam would just say, "That's what I want, that's what I want!" And so, you found a way to do it. You invented things, ways to get around problems, to give him what he was looking for.

Sam felt — and he was right — that the longer you make the shot, the better the people can act it out, the more real it all seems, instead of making it in small pieces — cut, cut, cut, the way it is usually done. And he wanted to make some of the pictures we did in about seven pieces of film. Instead of having the usual sixty or eighty pieces of film. So we would have these long, long takes, and you're on the dolly and going through two different rooms and people coming in and out and down hallways and things like that.

These shots had to be well-planned, really well-planned. We would re-hearse for a day, or three-fourths of a day, and then we'd shoot the scene. It took me some time to light these shots, to light the different places, the different rooms. And the other guys had just as many problems. The sound men had a helluva time with some of these long scenes, moving from set to set. Up in the rafters, over the floor, where we hang the lights we had about three guys up there just waving mikes around, because they couldn't be down on the floor — there was no place to put them that the camera wasn't going to pass by. So they would all be up there with fishpoles — aluminum piping with a microphone at the end — bending and swinging them back and forth. And the sound mixer had a helluva time because he couldn't see what was going on, he didn't know where anybody was. The camera was going down the hallways, out of sight.

The most complicated shot we ever did was on *Forty Guns.* Sam had a scene he wanted to shoot in one take — the actors are inside, they come out, they go down the street, stop, talk, go in and out, and finally some horses go riding by. The shot went from the bottom of the hill all the way up to the top of the hill. We shot it a couple of times, but we found that the dirt road was too rough for the crane. The crane arm with the camera, thirty feet out on the arm of the crane, was just bouncing all over the place. We couldn't shoot it. We realized to shoot it we were going to have to lay track — a thousand feet, eleven hundred feet of track. That's a big project, laying eleven hundred feet of double-boarded track. It was about eleven o'clock, and we had shot it a couple of times and it was no good. We called the construction gang in and told them what we had to do. The guy said, "No problem, no problem." Hell, they brought about fifty guys. And they laid the track down. To start with they brought a big scraper and scraped down the street so they wouldn't have to use too much of what we call "cribbing," wedges that you put in between the dirt and the tracks to keep it even. Then they put down the double-boarded track. It had to be two boards for something like this, with a crane. You lay one board down, a two-by-twelve, another two-by-twelve down on top of it, separate the ends of it so they don't come together and you get bumps.

So they had it all down — one thousand one hundred feet of it — by one-thirty in the afternoon. We put the crane on and ran it up and down a couple of times, and at two o'clock we shot it. We got it the first take. A thing like that is so damned expensive to do and it's going to run so damn long in the picture that you just can't shoot one take, you have to have a safety in case something happens. But that whole long shot, I don't think we did more than two takes. And that was it.

Run of the Arrow was the first picture I did with Sam. We made it all up in Utah. Rod Steiger was an uncooperative actor. That is an understatement. You have to know him — such a goddamned egotist and everything had to be done his way. And Sam was a head-and-a-half shorter than Steiger, but he wasn't going to get the best of Sam. And a short fellow in this business can have more ego than a guy eight feet tall. Sam just made Steiger do what he wanted. He'd say, "I don't give a goddamn whether you like it or not, you're gonna do it my way!" And Steiger was just as obstinate. He was going to do it his way. We had a long dolly shot with men on horseback and the cavalry coming down the street. We started about seven-thirty, eight o'clock in the morning with the first take, and by eleven thirty Steiger hadn't done it the way Sam wanted it. And now Steiger was really screaming and yelling. And Sam says, "Look, you're gonna do it my way or we're gonna stay here till the goddamn moon comes up. But you're gonna do it my way." And that was it. And then he said, "Okay, lunch." It was only eleven thirty. So we went to lunch and came back and did it some more, and we finally did it Sam's way. And that's the way that whole picture went with Steiger.

We had some long takes in *Run of the Arrow*. The scene in the tent ran about six hundred or seven hundred feet. We spent a whole day on it because Sam wanted it all in one take. This wasn't difficult to shoot, no problems for the camera. But the worst part of long scenes is you don't have any control over it. If there's a mistake you have to start over. And when you have to go back over a long take it gets monotonous. The crew was fed up with it, they were fed up with Steiger. And he would blow his lines a couple of times, and just go back and pick it up from there, not from the beginning, and it started throwing the girl off, too. And the retakes gradually got slower and slower. The more we did it the worse it got. So one of the early takes had to be used for the picture, with the mistakes in it. But when you have one take there's nothing to cut away from when there's a mistake. You're in trouble. But Sam found a way to do it. He put the film in the optical printer, enlarged it and used one side of the film or the other side as if they were different shots — which can be lousy because you get these funny close profiles.

There was a problem with the Mexican girl in *Run of the Arrow*. They just couldn't understand her. And there was an up and coming gal that Sam knew, Angie Dickinson, and Sam got her to redub the whole damn picture with her voice. It took a long time and Sam said, "I'll pay you back, don't worry." And so when he made *China Gate* he gave her the lead part. Angie was very good in it but it took her a long time to get herself established. Nat "King" Cole was in that, and he was a great guy, a wonderful guy. When you get around these stars for ten or twelve hours a day you see their real selves, and a few of them are damn nice people.

China Gate was supposed to be in Asia, in the jungles and rivers, but we didn't have enough money to go anywhere so we did it all in the studio. The sets were all borrowed sets — what they call "standing sets" — and they had to be changed around a lot to look like it was Vietnam or wherever the goddamn thing took place. And we did it very fast. And I did one more picture with Sam, *Verboten* — Christ, that picture was made in ten, eleven days. And both of those pictures must have gone smooth because I can't remember a damn thing about them and you remember only the things that go wrong.

We talked about doing a big war picture a long time back. Matter of fact, he's got some pictures I took in the war of the camps where the Germans burned up the prisoners. I loaned them to Sam and he took them all over the world and I'm still waiting to get them back.

Sam was a helluva nice guy. I got along fine with him. Great to work with, full of ideas, and a great storyteller.

Gene Fowler, Jr.

Film Editor: *Run of the Arrow, China Gate, Forty Guns*

I was working on a picture at RKO, the name of which escapes me, and Sam came in and asked me if I wanted to work on his picture, *Run of the Arrow*. It turned out he knew my father from the old days on the New York newspapers. And based on that he thought maybe I could cut his picture!

My old man and Sam got together and would break bread. And I loved Sam, we got along great, although the picture was a long, hard grind.

They were up in St. George, Utah, and shipping the film back here to Hollywood. And at one point I started getting this shot of the covered wagons. The camera would go along this line of covered wagons, an actor in the distance would wave or something, and then the wagons would disappear over the horizon. Over and over, four hundred, five hundred foot rolls of film, all shot silent. And in each take the camera would be panning smoothly and then suddenly the camera would *jerk*. Each take the same thing, the camera would make this sudden jerking motion. This was my first picture with Sam and I didn't know what to make of it. I went up to St. George right after that and I asked the camera operator about it. "What the hell was wrong with the camera on that covered wagon shot? Every time at the same point the camera jerks." It turned out that Sam — who dressed up for his westerns with a six-shooter and a ten-gallon hat — would shoot a gun as an actor's cue — the actor was far away in the covered wagon and when he wanted the actor to do something he would shoot the gun. But he would shoot it right next to the camera operator's ear and the camera would jump each time he did it.

Sam was intimidating to a lot of people. I remember something that happened when they were shooting *China Gate*. Sam is a guy who shoots very long scenes, no cuts, and he usually shoots just one take. So if anything turned out to be wrong with the take you were screwed. They were shooting this scene, a long one, and at the end of it the actor gets riddled with machine guns and he's filled with squibs where the bullets are supposed to be hitting. And the long scene started and I heard this ticking sound. The goddamned tick was almost rhythmical and I kept looking at the sound man and I said, "Don't you hear it? Shouldn't you tell them to cut?" And he kept brushing me off. And finally the squibs went off and it was the end of the scene. And I said, "What the hell was that ticking?" Well, it turned out to be the fog machine, and as it squirted out some fog it made a big click. I asked the sound man, "Why the hell didn't you stop the take?" And he said, "Well, Sam told me never to stop the take while it's under way." I said, "Well, that's ridiculous. Didn't you hear that ticking?" He said, "No, I didn't hear a thing." And so they had to make another take, and had to resquib the actor and everything and this whole long routine and it could have been saved by this dumb bastard saying we had to stop and kick the fog machine. And unfortunately the first take ended up being the only usable one and so we had to use it and go through the entire sound track and cut out each of these fog machine ticks.

But Sam could do that to people, if you didn't know him. You know how he talks — he's not a shy man at all. And people could be intimidated. And he could do it to producers, too. And that was in the days before directors had halos and could do no wrong and had the last word. In those days it was the producer who took charge. But Sammy could handle producers. If they disagreed with him he could cast doubts in their minds that they were wrong. He always got what he wanted and did things the way he wanted to do them.

You could be easily intimidated by him, and I think sometimes actors did things for him they had no business doing. In *Forty Guns,* Barbara Stanwyck agreed to do a scene where she's dragged by a horse, her foot is caught in the stirrup and the horse drags her all over. I said to him, "You're out of your bloody mind, Sam, for Christ sake! What if something happens? You've still got days to go with her in the picture! You got the star there!" And he said, "Well, I asked her and she said she'd do it."

And there was the dust storm with Stanwyck and the other lead, and Sam used cement instead of dust. They blew it through the wind machine. Have you ever breathed *cement?* Normally they would use a certain kind of dirt. But you know I think Sam didn't want to use that because it had his name, "Fuller's earth" it's called. So he had them use cement. And Jesus Christ, when you get cement in your eyes . . . it was dreadful! But Sam liked Stanwyck for doing it—she was a real trouper from way back—and he couldn't speak highly enough of her.

In the beginning when I worked with him Sam would have a lot of input in the cutting. And then when he decided I knew what I was doing I could do almost anything I wanted. As I said, Sam liked to do these long, uncut scenes, and doesn't do a lot of takes. So if an actor would flub a line in the middle of a take it presented quite a problem for me because you had nothing to cut away to. I really don't know why they wouldn't retake these scenes with the flubbed lines in them. I don't know if Sam figured something could be done about it later or if he didn't hear it. Sam is a writer, but on the set I think he's a visual man and when he's watching the thing going I don't think he hears the dialogue. And the actors wouldn't stop—sometimes you don't know that you've made a flub.

So this was a problem. I had to figure out how the hell to get this flub out of the shot without butchering it. I had a friend by the name of Linwood Dunn, who was the head of the optical department. And he and his partner had developed this machine, and they knew it backwards and forwards, could do magic with it. And I went to them and told them my problem. I knew that we could do an optical zoom in, but what I didn't like about a zoom was that it starts off at full speed in one frame and then it stops at full speed to normal in one frame. It's not like a dolly and I told them I wanted to make this optical look like a dolly, start up, get to speed, then slow down and stop. And we figured out how to do it, to make a zoom look like a dolly. And if you look at *China Gate,* you'll see how we dealt with a lot of these sustained scenes, moving into a closeup and then cutting back to the long shot. And as a matter of fact they're rather interesting to look at. It worked out pretty well. But I learned more about the optical screen department with that film than I ever wanted to know.

On *Run of the Arrow* the scene I remember the most was the fight at the end of the picture. Sam had really shot film for that, thousands and thousands of feet of film of this damn battle. This was a difficult scene to cut. And one of the things when you have a tremendous amount of film is not to be overwhelmed by it, but to divide it into sections, so that it is not just a mishmash of film but each element is coherent to the audience and leads to the next thing. And that was all that was left to be edited, and I got a call, a fellow wanted to know if I wanted to direct a picture. So I went to Sam and I said, "Look, I've got an offer to direct a picture. How about it?" He said, "Go ahead, I'll have your assistant put the thing together." So I went off and directed this picture, *I Was a Teenage Werewolf.* And I finished my picture and came back about six weeks later and they were still screwing around with this battle. They were overwhelmed by all the film, and my assistant was overwhelmed by Sam and would do anything Sam told him to do. And it is easy to get confused with so much film and you can't hold it all in your mind. So I took the thing and figured out an approach—let's do what Sam keeps yelling about with a modern battle, big preparation, execution and aftermath, breaking it into these three sections. And we put the thing together and Sam liked it.

It was during the making of *Run of the Arrow* that I first heard Sam planning *The Big Red One.* And he would act the scenes out for you, the action, the dialogue, the whole thing. He'd get very excited about it, and I must have heard the opening to the picture about twenty-two times. But it took twenty-some years before he got to make it. I was at Lorimar at that time when Sam showed up, and he was going to make *Big Red One.* It was budgeted at fourteen million dollars, which was a large budget then—of course today it's nothing at all—and Sam had the cooperation of the Army and some generals in Washington were going to let him have the armaments and so on. But Lorimar was notoriously cheap in its own stupid way, and they said that was too expensive. So they re-budgeted it and cut a lot of the heart out of it. And Sam, who is the eternal optimist, said, "Don't worry, I can make it. I'll have the big battle offstage, all sound effects." And it didn't turn out as well as it should have, but he got it made.

Sam has that incredibly positive attitude. He's a unique movie director, an unpolished stone, full of energy and ideas—the most fertile mind! You can say to Sam, "Give me an idea for a picture." And Sam will tell you standing up. He'll start telling a story—he doesn't know where it's going but he'll make it go. He's a tremendous character.

Constance Towers
Actor: *Shock Corridor, The Naked Kiss*

I was introduced to Sam at a party at Barry Sullivan's house. We talked a while, and Sam said he was going to make a movie called *Shock Corridor* and asked if I would be interested in playing the feminine lead in it. I really didn't know very much about Sam, but Barry Sullivan—whom I respect highly—said that Sam was one of the greatest film directors that he knew, a very talented man, innovative and exciting to work with. So, soon after I got hold of a couple of Sammy's films and I looked at them and decided that I would work with him. And so we did *Shock Corridor*. And right after that we made *The Naked Kiss* together.

Sammy was a great actor's director. He gave the actors a tremendous amount of confidence, inspired you to go ahead and try what you felt about your character. He'd say, "I'll let you know if I don't like it." He let you be part of the creative process. He gave you freedom in your acting, which was wonderful. And at the same time you trusted him to tell you if it was wrong or right. Because if it wasn't right for the character he was very honest and he would tell you. You didn't have to try and guess what Sammy was thinking or feeling about something. He let you know. And I think his films reflect his style on the set—they're very open, very candid, spontaneous. But at the same time he always knows where he's going in the end. He knows exactly what he's trying to say. And if you miss it he will tell you again at the end, with a wonderful little quote.

The Naked Kiss particularly had a number of difficult scenes, complicated emotional situations for the character, and it would have been very difficult if he had been one of those directors who wouldn't—or couldn't—explain a scene to you. But you were taken by the hand by Sammy at those moments, so you knew where you were. Sammy was right there with you in every scene, taking every breath with you, living every moment. And as I say, if you dug down and found something deeper in the scene, in your character, he was thrilled to death. He was like Hitchcock or Ford, everything was well planned before he started, but he was open to something spontaneous or a new idea. Even using the song that was in *The Naked Kiss*. That was a song I had sung before and he heard it and thought it would be wonderful in the picture. And that's how that song came to be in the picture. We were on very short schedules, because these were low-budget films, but Sammy always found time to talk to you if you had a question or a suggestion. I could call him at any time I wanted to talk, and I would go over to his house and have lunch and we would talk about any questions I might have. And I can't tell you what a luxury that is for an actor.

I think the most difficult thing I did in those two films was the first scene in *The Naked Kiss*. Sammy discussed with me exactly what we were trying to accomplish in that first moment. We were going to show a horrifying side of this woman who had gotten into an ugly predicament. The character was a "hooker with a heart," but in that opening scene we see her at her worst. She's fighting for her life—this man had been mistreating her, had shaved her head. And she goes wild, beats him, beats him to the ground and takes her money from him. And that was going to be the opening scene in the movie.

It was a difficult scene to do. Not from the acting standpoint. As a woman, it was not hard to find your own sources to do the scene, to feel the rage against this man for what he had done to her. There was quite enough in the situation to work on for an actress. But the scene was technically very difficult.

I was most concerned when I heard that she was going to be bald in the scene — her wig is torn off in the fight and you find out that her head has been shaved bald. I wanted to know what he was going to do with that, because Sammy liked the scenes to be very real. But he said, "No, you'll be all right, we'll put a skullcap on you." And they very carefully worked on a skullcap so it did look like my own flesh. You have to wonder how you're going to look in a scene like that, but luckily we had Stanley Cortez as the cinematographer, who had probably photographed women as beautifully as anyone in the history of the business. And Stanley liked women, he liked women's faces, and he was just splendid. Then I wondered how much they wanted me to show, because I wasn't going to do it nude and with that skullcap on! But he said, "No, we won't show all of you." And it was like the striptease scene we did in *Shock Corridor,* and Sammy said, "You create an illusion. It's not what you see, it's what you think you see."

The scene was already shocking and the way it was shot made it doubly shocking. We had hand-held cameras strapped on to the cameraman, and I was hitting directly into the camera. And when you watch that you really feel like you are the person being beaten up.

Actually, the person who got beat up for real in that film was Virginia Grey. And it was a terrible thing, because I loved her so much — such a wonderful actress and a wonderful human being. And in the scene when I hit her with my purse, Sammy said, "*Really* hit her now." And Virginia said, "Yes, *really* hit me." And, well, I did. And I guess I was still green, I didn't realize that when she said "really hit me" she meant in a stage way, not full force. And I really whacked her. So what you see in the film is an honest reaction on her part. And poor Virginia didn't tell me for a long time afterward that she went around with a jaw that ached so badly after that. And I apologized for many years, every time I saw her. I always put my arms around her and said, "Virginia, forgive me!"

These were brutal films for that time. They showed a very different side of life than people were used to seeing on the screen in that period. And you realize now how Sammy was so far ahead of everybody. Stories of sexual abuse of children are all over the news today, but back then no one talked about that kind of horrifying reality. It was very courageous of him to take those stories and tell them as honestly as he did.

Sammy himself had a wonderful side to him when he was around children.

Constance Towers and Anthony Eisley in an early scene from *The Naked Kiss* (1964). Note that the paperback Towers is reading is an edition of Fuller's *The Dark Page*.

There was no one who was more sensitive, tender, and almost childlike with a child. He came over to my house and met my children when they were little. And he was just wonderful, such a delight with the children. It was a side to him that you just wouldn't expect.

When we made these films they were, as I said, ahead of their time. But when I was in Paris some time later I found out that the films were well known. *Shock Corridor* had played in Paris for five years! And I would walk down the streets in Paris and I would be stopped very often by people who had seen that one or *Naked Kiss*. And then I guess when I really found out the impact these films had was in New York when I was doing *The King and I* with Yul Brynner. And one night a few of the Kennedy boys and Andy Warhol all came to see the play, and they came backstage afterward. They were sitting in my dressing room and Andy Warhol said to me, "I have to tell you, I'm awed to meet you because you were in my two favorite films, *Shock Corridor* and *Naked Kiss*." And I thought, my gosh! But I have met many others who, like Andy Warhol, worshipped Sammy. And when I have gone to meet a producer or young directors today the first thing they want to tell me is, "I saw your work with Sammy Fuller." And they want to know about him—he's their hero.

Sammy, in private, is a very mysterious person. I don't know many people who know Sammy very well. He's very difficult to know. But if you are his friend, you are really his friend and you are kind of accepted to an inner place in his life. One person who did know Sammy that way, and had great respect for him, was John Ford. John Ford would come to the set to watch Sammy working. He was there practically every day, sitting and watching. He would say, "Maybe I can learn something." John Ford was also a great personal friend to me, as well as a film director I worked with on several films, and we would have tea together. Every afternoon the three of us and whoever was there would stop and have tea—and it was really tea!—and cookies.

Sammy is a real storyteller, that's what he lives for. I don't think he ever thought about the commercial side of a thing. I don't think money had any appeal to him. He was not ostentatious in any way. He lived simply, and his house was just a little old bungalow in Hollywood. And there was not one inch of wall space inside that wasn't crammed full of books. He was always talking about a new project, a new story he was researching or writing. He was an insatiable reader, and I always had the feeling that all of his private hours were spent reading, researching, hungering for more knowledge. He was always the newspaperman, always on the scent of a new story. That is Sammy's passion!

Adam Greenberg

Director of Photography: *The Big Red One*

I had been working only on Israeli movies, and one American co-production made in Israel, *The Passover Plot*. Gene Corman, who was producing *The Big Red One*, had seen this and thought I could do the photography for their movie. I was working in Israel on another movie and I got the message:

they wanted me for an American movie, with Lee Marvin, to be shot in Israel, and directed by Sam Fuller.

I knew a little bit about Sam Fuller. I knew some of his movies and it was very exciting to meet him. He came to Israel to scout locations and we met. And I thought he was an amazing and very funny man. Great fun to be with.

We scouted locations all over Israel, and then we were to go to Yugoslavia for more location scouting. We flew to Italy and then we were supposed to fly to Belgrade. I was carrying an Israeli passport and at that time Israel had no diplomatic relationship with Yugoslavia. So Gene Corman had to make a special arrangement for me to have a visa, and this visa would be at the airport in Belgrade. But it happened that our plane made a stop in Zagreb, Yugoslavia, and all the passengers had to step out and have their passports inspected. Of course, I did not have a visa—it was waiting for me in Belgrade. So they said, "You go to jail." So I was arrested and spent twenty-four hours in the Zagreb jail. Gene Corman and Sam had to fly to Belgrade and straighten this out so the police would let me go. And they were a little worried because their cameraman was now in a Yugoslav jail. And as it happened we never shot those scenes in Yugoslavia, it didn't work out. We shot everything in Israel except for some scenes done in Ireland.

Actually, we almost had the same thing happen when we went to Ireland, after eight weeks shooting in Israel. We were going to shoot some European scenes, the fall of Berlin and things. Gene Corman chartered a plane to fly us to Dublin, with all of the artillery and ammunition and explosives, all the props to continue the film. And it was all arranged for us to bring these things into the country. And there was very bad weather when we took off and the pilot finally says, "We can't land in Dublin, the weather is too rough, we have to land in another city." And Gene and Sam were thinking what happened in Yugoslavia when we landed in the wrong city, and here we are on a plane filled with weapons and explosives and Gene Corman says, "If we land somewhere else we'll *all* go to jail! You have to land in Dublin, fog or no fog!" And he forced the pilot to land in the bad weather—it was a charter, you know.

On the first day of shooting I came with some of the light Arriflex cameras and Sam had never seen this kind of camera. You must remember that he had not made a film in some years at that time and many things had changed. And he asked me, "You're going to shoot with this?" He thought it was a home movie camera or something. I said, "This is a sound camera. Thirty-five millimeters." And Sam did not want to use multiple cameras for scenes. One camera only. He staged everything for one camera. He allowed us to use other cameras—you know, this was a war movie, with lots of action and equipment, and it is normal to cover this with multiple cameras. But Sam knew what he needed and staged everything for one camera. And we would go to see the dailies and he only watched what was from this one camera. He didn't even want to see the other film. He said, "It's okay, keep watching. The rest is for you guys"—for Gene Corman and me. For Sam, just one camera. And I respected this very much. He had made many great films and this was how he did it. A single camera and many single takes as well. This was incredible for me, these long scenes. This was a big war situation and it was incredible just to watch, to see how he staged these scenes. It was not like a movie, you know, it was like it was really happening right in front of you. His staging of these war scenes was incredible!

He was an incredibly visual director. He could stage things, one image that would take three or four pages to describe. I remember one setup that was supposed to be at the concentration camp in Czechoslavkia. In the front a few GIs are sitting under a tree. And in the background you see a big line of German prisoners.

It is a wide angle, the prisoners crossing from left to right in the background. And they keep coming, these prisoners. It looks like they go on forever. And at the very end you see one American soldier with a gun. One man who has the bullets controls all those men.

I don't know what age Sam was when he was doing *The Big Red One*. Close to seventy, you say? I was maybe forty years old and he was much stronger than me. In such good shape, full of energy. And full of stories, always the stories. He would use guns to cue the action. We were filming at long distances and he would shoot these guns to cue the actors. And he was standing right behind me and the camera, because I was operating the camera. Standing behind my head, bending over with the cigar in the mouth and firing these two guns like a cowboy—bang! bang! bang! And there was always somebody standing by to reload bullets in the gun. Never a boring day with Sam!

Sam's first cut of the movie ran six hours. I didn't see it. I was told it was the best cut of all. But a six-hour movie, it would never be released. You have to be realistic. Then they made a four-hour cut. I came to Los Angeles and I saw Sam's four-hour cut. It was an incredible movie. No question at all. And then the studio took it away from Sam, he was replaced. They put their own editor on the picture and he cut it down, and it went back and forth, and it was now under two hours and that is the movie that is left. I still like the movie very much. But it is not as good as Sam's cut. The longer cut was a very great movie.

You really don't find any directors like Sam Fuller any more. I have worked with many major figures since then—and this movie opened a lot of doors for me, led to many other things—but you don't find anyone like Sam Fuller. I would work with him today on anything, anywhere. He is obviously a great director, a brilliant filmmaker and an honorable man. I love him and I will remember him for all my life.

Karl Lewis Miller
Dog Trainer: *White Dog*

I first heard the story of *White Dog* more than twenty years ago. I read it in *Life* magazine, a true story by Romain Gary. As I recall it, Jean Seberg found the dog, and one time it attacked their black gardener and hurt him quite badly. Then they put the dog up around people but one time they didn't put him up and he bit someone else that happened to be black. And they came to realize that the dog didn't bother anyone but black people. And this was factual. The movie took some dramatic license and changed things around, but this was basically a true story. They did this in the South, they could train dogs to attack only black people, and they were known as "white dogs."

Many years after I read that story I got a call from Paramount. They were going to make the movie. I was in Hawaii, working with the dogs for *Magnum P.I.*, the first season for the show, and the network wouldn't guarantee a pickup for the next season. So I told Paramount I would do *White Dog*. I didn't know *Magnum P.I.* would be a hit. I could have been in Hawaii for seven years!

So when Sam came on the picture I had already been hired to start putting the animal work together. The Paramount brass who hired me wanted a white German shepherd to go along with the title, and when Sam came on he thought that was a mistake. He wanted a dark shepherd because the title referred to race, not to the color of the dog. The executive at Paramount just thought, "white dog," *white* German shepherd. So there was talk about making a change, but the feeling was that I was already so far with the training that, well, we've come this far, let's stay with what we've got.

Working with Sam on that picture was a real learning experience for me. It wasn't him telling me what to do or how to work my dogs. It was a case of telling me what he wanted to portray and finding ways to give him what he wanted to portray and finding ways to give him what he wanted. This was going to be an important animal picture with a strong statement and he was very concerned that the dogs performed well and that the violence looked real. At the same time he was very concerned that we didn't hurt any of the animals at any time. There were a few specific things he wanted from the dogs.

First, as he described it to me, he didn't want to show a dog that looked trained — that is, where the dog is in the center of a scene and you know that it's looking at a trainer beside the camera telling him what to do. And this really led me to pinpoint my own specialty in this business, and that is training dogs to look untrained. It's similar to the looseness in the training of seeing-eye dogs. First they are trained in military style, mechanical, strict obedience routine. But after basic training they're allowed to *not* obey and become looser, more natural looking. So then when a blind person might demand that the seeing-eye dog go forward, the seeing-eye dog goes, "Whoa, wait a minute, traffic's coming, I'm not going forward for you." So they're taught what we call "clever disobedience." And to give Sam what he wanted, we had to do this. You tell the dog to sit, stay, and then kind of wander off the set as if you didn't care, and allow the dog to continue on his own—actually to respond to the scene like an actor. And putting this together was a learning experience for me and Sam was a great teacher.

Then another thing he wanted was spectacular leaping attacks. And this was another thing I developed for *White Dog* and have used a lot since then. You see, normally when a dog attacks, like a wolf, it will run straight at you, climb up the guy's chest and grab for the face or the arm in front of the face. But Sam wanted spectacular leaps from several yards away onto the guy, knock him right down and bite him all over. So we had to build ramps, eight foot ramps tapering up to three feet high, and train the dogs to climb up the ramp and leap off, go through the air and hit the guy. And as the guy would fall over to stay on him and maul the guy all over. Sam wanted that, and we developed it and I've used it ever since.

And there was something else Sam wanted me to do. He said, "The dog looks good, he's attacking real nice, but that tail is wagging like he's having fun!" But all dogs attack with the tails up and wagging. It's like a rudder, for balance. Even a bad dog or a police dog, they all attack that way. But in a movie, in a scene of violence, it's true, the tail up and wagging takes away a degree of viciousness. So for certain shots where the tail was wagging too much we tied it down with a hidden string, under the legs and tied to the belly. It didn't hurt the animal, it was just a collar around the tail. That was one thing about Sam, he never wanted any animal getting hurt. And I remember once, we were in the midst of setting up a shot for a brutal animal attack and the grips were clearing the debris from the location. They picked up a piece of old, dirty plywood and underneath was a nest of a mother mouse and her little baby mice. And they would have cleared them out of there and Sam looked at the baby mice and said, "Don't disturb 'em. We'll shoot somewhere else."

The most difficult scene we did for that picture I can tell you without even stopping to think about it. This was a scene early in the picture where Kristy McNichol is asleep in her bedroom, and the dog is asleep in another part of the house, and an intruder comes in and sneaks through the hallway and goes in to try and rape her, they wrestle, she gets away from him and then the dog comes into it, attacks the rapist, chases him and crashes through the glass window to get the guy before he escapes. And Sam wanted to do this all in one shot. One master shot! Everyone said it couldn't be done and by God he did it. It blew my mind! It blew everyone's mind.

The shot starts with a blasting war movie on the TV screen and the camera pulls back to show the dog sleeping, eyes closed and sound asleep with the war movie blasting in his ear, so he can't hear anyone sneaking into the house. Now the camera starts down the hallway—it was a steadycam, hand-held by the operator—looks in Kristy's room, goes back out to the hallway and reveals the rapist is there—which is played by me. I played the intruder in the picture. Then the camera looks over my shoulder as I get to Kristy's room and peek inside. And I go in and grab her, we wrestle, I tackle her to the ground and the dog leaps into frame and starts attacking me. The dog's tearing me up but I get away and run out the door, slamming the door closed behind me, and the camera shows the dog, bewildered, and then the dog looks at the window and it leaps right through the glass window, crashes onto the ground and catches the guy—me—before I can get away. And that son-of-a-gun did it all in one take. One take and three different dogs.

See, that's the only way we could do it and get all those different actions with the camera running all the time. The first dog was on cue to keep his head down and close his eyes—he wasn't really asleep, he was just trained to act asleep. Now, as the camera left him and went down the hallway, the other trainer took that dog out and brought up the second dog when the camera was on me chasing Kristy McNichol, and the trainer released that dog to attack me. Then, as I escaped through the door, they lined up the third dog who only did the jump through the glass window and jumped on me on the outside. Each dog knew only his piece of the trick. One dog knew to lie down, eyes closed. The next dog knew only to leap on me and bring me down. The third dog knew only to leap through the glass window. And we did it all, one take, a beautiful shot. I think we did it three times. Each take had some minor flaw in the camera moves, or a beat off in the timing, and he had to shoot some coverage. We couldn't do it again after three takes because the dogs would be burned out. But each of the three takes was usable. It was a great, great shot, and an impossible feat! But Sam, you know, the thing about him is he really knew in his mind what he wanted and he had to get it. I mean, he was really steadfast in what he wanted to accomplish in every scene.

For a film like this you had to have multiple dogs. The work load was so heavy you needed multiple dogs for insurance, to guarantee that production would shoot on schedule without worrying that a dog tired out or refused to work. So we had about four dogs playing the White Dog. None of them were related, either. But you would never know from watching the picture that you were seeing a number of dogs on the screen. But Sam was a considerate man, very respectful to his employees. He did something, the only time I've seen it done—and I've been working on movies for twenty-seven years now: at the end of the movie, he gave each dog that worked on the picture a screen credit. Folsom, Heinz, Buster and Duke each got his name up there on the screen.

Larry Cohen

Writer-Director: *Return to Salem's Lot*

I have a house in Coldwater Canyon in Beverly Hills. I bought it some years ago from a cowboy actor named Clint Walker. The place was actually built in 1929 by George Hearst, the son of William Randolph Hearst, and it's a very big mansion. One day John Ireland was up here to read for a part. He was looking around and he said, "I've been here before. Sam Fuller owned this house." That was the first inkling I'd had that Sam Fuller had lived in the house. Some time later I was at a party at the Beverly Hills Hotel. It was a party for the French movie, *Cousin, Cousine,* and there were a lot of French people there and a lot of Americans who had lived in France. Sam was there and I met him. And I said, "Did you ever live up on Coldwater Canyon?" He said, "Yeah, big old house." I said, "Well, I think I've got your old house." He said, "My God! I'd love to show it to my wife. Could I come over some time?" This was his second wife, Christa. I think he may have lost the house when he got divorced from his first wife. And I said, "Sure, come on over." And he came over to the house, and we became very good friends as a result of all that.

We would see each other out here or when I went to Paris we would have dinner together and hang out. And at one point I decided I was going to write a part for Sam in one of my movies. The part I wrote for him was in *Return to Salem's Lot.* The character is an old guy who's been on the trail of a big Nazi war criminal, and he's scouring New England for him. He's a tough old guy and he carries a big gun with him—he says, "I'm not a Nazi hunter, I'm a Nazi *killer!*" And he comes into this small New England town searching for this big Nazi and finds instead that the secret residents of the town are not Nazis but vampires. And Michael Moriarty, who plays a young guy trying to fight these vampires, asks Sam's character to be his ally. The Nazi hunter knows all about the vampire folklore because his ancestors are from Central Europe. And he decides to help Moriarty fight them. Because he knows that vampires exist. He says, "People don't believe there are really vampires . . . and in a thousand years people won't believe there were Nazis!" So they team up and together they knock off the vampires. And at the end of the story they all drive off together to hunt for the Nazi.

I called Sam up and told him I had written this part for him in *Return to Salem's Lot* and I asked him if he wanted to do it. He said, "Sure!" So I sent him the script. Then he called me up and said, "Jeez, there's an awful lot of lines! I didn't know I was gonna talk so much in this part." He was used to doing a day here or a day there, a cameo appearance for directors that liked him. But this was a fully integrated part in the script and he had to be around for at least four weeks.

We flew him over—we shot it in New York and then up in Vermont. And Sam was still a little worried about it when we started because of all the lines of dialogue and blocking and he even had to do a couple of stunts—falls and fights and all of that. But he was perfect for the part, and he enjoyed himself. People ask whether it was difficult directing another director. I had directed other actors who were directors and I always find that they are the most cooperative because they know what you're up against and as long as they sense you know what you're doing they don't interfere and they try to give you just what you want from them. And that's how it was with Sam. He was tremendously easy to deal with. And we worked long, long hours and all through the night—it was a vampire movie so you had to shoot most of it at night. Sometimes we wouldn't start until seven o'clock in the evening and then we'd shoot until two or three the next afternoon. Crazy hours. An actor might not be needed until twelve midnight. And Sam was always ready, well-groomed, alert and full of pep. And actually, it was great to have someone Sam's age there because it kept all the younger people in line. It was difficult to complain about the hours and the work when Sam was around, looking so energetic.

The only problem I had was with those damned cigars of Sam's. Every time we put a radio mike on Sam we got terrible static. Everybody was going crazy trying to figure out what was wrong with the radio mikes. Finally, I fired the sound man because I thought his equipment was no good, we had to get somebody else up there. Then another sound man came up, put the radio mikes on Sam and again we got the static. We couldn't believe it! Everyone else's radio mike worked. We tried switching mikes around. Finally, I was ready to fire the second sound man and I said to Sam, "Do you know anything that could be causing this? Anything in your pockets that could be causing the static?" He says, "No. All I've got in my pockets are cigars." He pulled open his jacket and there were three cigars tucked in each inside pocket. And what we'd been hearing through the mikes was the rustling of the cellophane on the cigars. I couldn't believe it! For three days we had the problem and he never suggested it might be his cigar wrappers. And I never asked him because I thought it would be an insult to ask something so obvious—he'd directed twenty-three pictures, after all. But it didn't dawn on him.

I didn't want him to smoke the cigars on-camera. I said to him, "Sam, if you're gonna smoke the cigars in the picture we're going to be in a lot of trouble because, you know, in one shot the cigar will be one length and in the next angle it will be short, and when we cut back it'll be long again, it will never match..." He said, "Oh *no, no,* don't worry about it! I'll take care of it, I'll keep an eye on the cigar in every shot." So, I left the cigar problem up to him, and sure enough in every cut the cigar was shorter, then it was longer, then the cigar was shorter again... He didn't keep an eye on it at all! So then cutting the picture was an agonizing experience, trying to find shots where

Sam Fuller as a Nazi vampire hunter in Larry Cohen's *Return to Salem's Lot* (1988).

the cigar was out of frame and matching it to the next shot, so there wasn't a big jump with the cigar growing and shrinking with every cut. It took *days* of extra editing time, finding alternate takes, and sometimes different bits of dialogue, trying to match lip movements, just to get rid of this fucking cigar! It was everything I had feared it was going to be — and worse. And at the time you couldn't help but laugh. I should have known better. But then again, trying to take a cigar away from Sam Fuller is like trying to take a bottle away from a baby. And of course every time I've gone to see him in the past I would bring him a box of cigars.

We shot *Return to Salem's Lot* in Vermont and New York. We found an old mansion in New York that was perfect — it's actually a museum — and we shot one scene in a park in Harlem. And Sam was full of stories about his old days in New York. He's a real New York character, and it surprised me to realize that he had never actually shot a film in New York. Even *Pickup on South Street* was all done in Los Angeles. I don't know why, since Fox at that time did a lot of crime pictures, *Kiss of Death* and others, on location in New York. And I hope that before he retires Sam will get to make at least one picture on the streets of New York.

I feel very affectionate towards Sam. We are good friends and I look forward to each time I go to Paris and see Sam, and we go to dinner and eat very good French food. Sam's a great guy.

Appendix A:
The Novels of Samuel Fuller

Aside from the career coda of autobiography, very few Hollywood movie directors have ever ventured into the lonely and financially tenuous world of book-writing, and fewer still have published works of fiction. Elia Kazan, Michael Crichton and John Sayles are among the small group of directors who have gone back and forth between storytelling on film and on the printed page. Sam Fuller has been writing novels since he was a reporter and all through his career as a filmmaker, and while their quality and value may vary greatly, each book offers at the least an interesting perspective on Fuller and his better-known works for the cinema.

Most of the later novels have their origins as screenplays. Some (*Crown of India, Quint's World*) are film projects Fuller never managed to get produced and eventually turned into prose. These novels offer a more elaborate and vivid word picture of the movies he might have made than one can get from reading the unproduced screenplays. The books published in conjunction with produced films (*The Naked Kiss, Dead Pigeon on Beethoven Street, The Big Red One*), fall into the disparaged category of "novelizations," paperbacks written to order from shooting scripts, publication timed to the release of the motion picture being adapted. Novelizations are normally assigned, for a flat fee, to fast paperback pros, such as mystery ace Michael Avallone, whose version of *Shock Corridor* for Belmont is one of the few such to be reprinted anywhere after a movie's original release. Rarely has a film director grabbed this minimal-prestige ancillary work, the pay — a few thousand dollars — being a pittance compared even to "B" movie money. But Fuller is an obsessive storyteller, and he undoubtedly takes pleasure in any opportunity to tell the tale one more time, regardless of medium or remuneration. In any case, Fuller's novelizations are not necessarily redundant — the paperback version of *The Big Red One*, written after the filming, contains enough material, by Fuller's own estimate, for a ten-hour movie.

His first novels were written and published while the author was still in his early twenties, still reporting crime for various newspapers. Although I

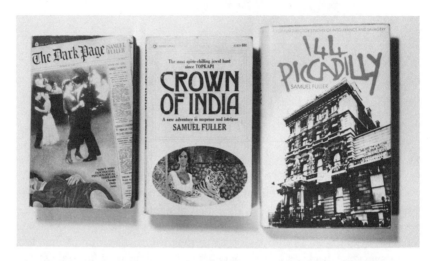

Top, from left to right: A 1982 edition of Fuller's most successful novel; a novelized version of an unproduced screenplay, in its original Award edition; the English hardcover edition of Fuller's "Swinging London" opus. *Bottom:* Three "paperback originals" adapted and expanded by Fuller from his screenplays; *Dead Pigeon* and *Big Red* were "movie tie-in" editions, but *Quint's World* (originally titled *Battle Royal*) has never been made as a film.

have been unable to track down copies of these first three books, from Fuller's description of their contents they were characteristic—provocative, tabloidish storylines drawn from real life, with elements of shock and surprise. *Burn, Baby, Burn* (1935) concerns the execution of a pregnant woman. *Test Tube Baby* (1936) is about experiments in artificial insemination and the world's first "ectogenic child." *Make Up and Kiss* (1938) is an exposé of the cosmetics industry.

The first was brought out by Phoenix Press, the other two by Godwin, both rock-bottom lending-library publishers that prospered during the Great Depression. According to bibliophile Bill Pronzini, chronicler of what he calls "alternative" literature, these fringe houses printed around two thousand copies of each title and paid the absolute minimum to their authors. Fuller recalls getting "a few hundred dollars" for all rights to the books, and this appears to be the high end of the pay scale. Pronzini, in his book *Gun in Cheek*, cites the case of Steve Fisher, future mystery novelist (*I Wake Up Screaming*) and screenwriter (*Lady in the Lake, Dead Reckoning*), who received exactly $125 for all rights to his first novel, published by Phoenix Press in 1935. Fuller says he wrote some other books for these lending-library houses, "under phony names," but their titles and everything else about them are lost to the ages.

Fuller's next known work of fiction, written after he had been writing screenplays in Hollywood for a few years, is *The Dark Page*. Published in 1944 by Duell, Sloan & Pearce, it is certainly the most successful and acclaimed of Fuller's novels. In it, he combines a tense and mood-drenched suspense story with an insider's look into the world of big city tabloid journalism. Although one of the first of its kind, the novel is an archetype of the *noir* style that thrived in print and film throughout the 1940s, from its shadowy atmosphere of New York streets at night to its delineation of the murderer's festering psychopathy.

The story of *The Dark Page* (curiously, perhaps even suspiciously, reminiscent of *The Big Clock* by Kenneth Fearing, written a few years later), involves a legendary tabloid newspaper editor, Carl Chapman, who, on the night of his greatest publicity stunt, a Lonely Hearts Ball at Madison Square Garden to be exploited by the paper, runs into a figure from his past, his first wife. When she threatens to destroy his present happiness, Chapman impulsively kills her. By chance, Chapman's star reporter, Lance McCleary, discovers her murder, and turns the hunt for her killer into circulation-boosting headlines. Chapman watches with mixed emotions as the investigation of the "Lonely Hearts Murder" increases sales while slowly uncovering his crime. To protect himself, he must kill again and again, and is finally forced to go gunning for McCleary, his protégé and a man he had looked upon as a son.

Fuller's plot is quite ingenious, with its weave of parallels and paradoxes: the investigation of one murder necessitates the commission of more murders; the man directing the investigation, Carl Chapman, is himself the murderer; he runs into his dreaded first wife at a convention of lonely unmarrieds. As he would do again and again in his films, Fuller here induces uncomfortable feelings of ambivalence toward his characters. Charlotte, the first murder victim, is an unbearable neurotic. Pop Farnsworth, the second victim, is a derelict drunkard and thief. Chapman, the bigamist and killer, is a devoted family man and a brilliant journalist. Because of their close relationship, hero McCleary's destruction of villain Chapman is a de facto act of betrayal (a situation echoed in *I Shot Jesse James, House of Bamboo* and *Underworld USA*). The hysteria of the climax leads to a melancholic postscript, as McCleary dumps the boss's body on the city desk and voices his sense of regret and culpability: "'He worked hard. All that counted was his wife and kids. She was a trespasser. Pop was a trespasser. Miller. I was a trespasser too. We wanted to take away his happiness. Look,' he said 'there's a hole in his belly.'"

The Dark Page plays out against the background of Park Row newspapers, Fuller's own world in the 1920s and early 1930s. Numerous elements in the book are drawn from his own experiences. Chapman's sensational newspaper, the *Comet,* is clearly based on the *Graphic,* where Fuller first worked as a crime reporter. The book's "Lonely Hearts Ball" was an actual promotion sponsored by the *Graphic* in January 1927 ("The *Graphic* swung wide open the gates of happiness last night," began the story in the next day's paper). The book's murderous editor, Carl Chapman, is strongly reminiscent of Emile Gauvreau, the tough and colorful editor of the *Graphic.* Fuller details one of the paper's most notorious practices, the use of "composite" photos, faked pictures of latebreaking news stories, and generally recreates the anything-goes attitude that made the meteoric *Graphic,* for a time, the world's most outrageous newspaper.

Fuller fills the book with the sights, sounds and smells of Lower Manhattan, particularly the low-life haven of the Bowery, with its pawnshops, flophouses, tattoo parlors and Salvation Army missions. Fuller's narrative tour of his old haunts is both harsh and nostalgic. The veteran of the crime beat is particularly effective in depicting the jaded indifference of metropolitan professionals who see murder and gore every working day. The visit to the morgue in Chapter Eight is a black-humored tour de force, from the jaunty greeting of Needle Nellie, who sews up corpses after the autopsies are completed, to the insouciant sports talk of Dr. O'Hanlon, the coroner:

> "You know, Lance, the Baltimore Orioles were the toughest bunch of players that ever got together." He sawed off the top of the skull and examined the brain. "Each one of 'em loved to scrap. That was when Johnnie McGraw played outfield..."

The Dark Page was published while Sam Fuller was in uniform, fighting his way across Europe. The book was widely reviewed, and received numerous good notices. Film rights were bought by Howard Hawks for $15,000. Hawks planned to use Edward G. Robinson and Humphrey Bogart as the editor and reporter. He never made the film and subsequently sold the rights—at a great profit—to Columbia. Retitled *Scandal Sheet,* the 1952 release starred Broderick Crawford as the editor and John Derek as the reporter.

There is a pause of 20 years between *The Dark Page* and the publication of Fuller's next novel, *The Naked Kiss.* He was understandably diverted from fiction, spending the two decades helping to liberate much of Europe, writing numerous produced and unproduced screenplays, and writing and directing 17 feature films. *Naked Kiss,* the novel, shows some of the usual flaws of a bastard form, with its original 100 pages or so of screenplay padded to 200-plus pages of prose with heaps of character backstory, and scenes Fuller imagined and staged for the camera losing their impact on the page. For example, the first paragraph of the novel's opening prologue reads this way: "Kelly was a beautiful prostitute. Even as she angrily attacked her drunken procurer with her handbag, the contortions could not shatter her elegance. Exquisitely filling a fitted sheath dress, the perfection of her figure matched that of her face." Compare that with the film's cold opening, the sudden, unexplained fury of the woman, snarling and smashing at the camera itself.

Crown of India, published in 1966 as a paperback original from Award Books, is a globe-trotting adventure story. The title refers to a fabulous and priceless diadem of precious stones, stolen en route from India to the World's Fair in New York. An international assortment of killers and thieves and a renegade insurance company executive try to profit from its recovery. Fuller, unleashed from the budgetary considerations of the cinema, fills the pages with spectacular locations and set pieces—white tiger hunt, camel stampede, Himalayan houseboats, the Maharajah's palace in Udaipur, a student riot in Cairo tossed in for a single paragraph of tangential color. The large cast is made up almost entirely of amoral and ruthless adventurers, although the hero, O'Meara, oddly for Fuller, is a conventional two-fisted leading man. More familiar is the marauding American villain, Ty Proctor, a spirited and imaginative sociopath, a lethal version of Skip McCoy from *Pickup on South Street.*

Motifs from the author's previous work pop up throughout the narrative. Kamela, the low-caste Indian, dreams of having a child with an American and letting it grow up in the United States, just like Lucky Legs in *China Gate.* There is a flashback to D-Day and references to Balzac and the Big Red One, a character goes to see *The Naked Kiss* at a New Delhi movie house, and the ending cribs the "father-son" confrontation and suicide climax from *The Dark Page.* Nonetheless, *Crown of India* is the least personal of Fuller's postwar books, an unresonant entertainment.

Fuller's next novel, *144 Piccadilly,* published in 1971, is unlike anything else he has ever done. The first person narrator, though never named (he

lets them call him Charlie; "It makes me think of a friendly bartender"), is
Fuller himself, American film director in London, fresh from a tribute in his
honor at the Edinburgh Film Festival and awaiting another at the National
Film Theatre. Returning to his hotel at dawn after a nostalgic stroll, the narrator runs into a cadre of hippies breaking into a four-story Georgian mansion
in Mayfair. They are squatters, part of a real-life London phenomenon of the
period, when activists and homeless hippies liberated unoccupied houses,
much to the violent outrage of the police and stodgier citizenry. Intrigued
("with a strange fascination bred in my days as a newspaper reporter in New
York"), the Fuller-figure finds himself participating in the illegal entry, and
gradually bridging the generational gap between his "beardless face and dull,
clean haberdashery" and their "freaked-out Bedouin menagerie." The hippies slowly turn their squat-house into a home, while fending off increasingly
violent incursions by police, the media, and brutal right-wing youth gangs.
Fuller, abandoning his suite at the Dorchester for a free-loving hippie chick
and a mattress on the floor, becomes the group's American mascot and hardboiled amanuensis. Although the squatters try to maintain an idealistic front
(no drugs and no public orgying!), events lead inevitably to violence, riot and
death.

    With its unrelenting counterculture lingo and flower power attitudiniz-
ing, the book seems very much a period piece, but it is no acid-era *Reefer
Madness*. Fuller actually does a great job of capturing the idealism, self-
absorption and giddy adventurism of the hippie phenomenon, and a point
in time when youth seemed a revolutionary force. Sociological interest aside,
Piccadilly provides hardcore Fuller buffs with a few bizarre kicks, as his
fictional incarnation roars around London on the back seat of a Hell's Angels
motorcycle, has wild sex with a beautiful squatter, beats up skinheads and
steals their steel-tipped boots, and gets shot up with heroin, twice!

    Dead Pigeon on Beethoven Street, published in 1974, is another paper-
back novelization. Without the film's arty stylization and playfulness the
story becomes a stripped-down, hardboiled thriller. A quick, entertaining
read, it at least serves to clear up or lend a bit of backstory to some of the film
version's confusing narrative.

    The revelation among Fuller's books is undoubtedly *The Big Red One*,
a novelization from the script of his 1980 film. The film version encountered
post-production interference. A four-hour cut by Fuller was brought down
to a modest 113 minutes, and a semi-folksy narration was foisted on the
soundtrack against Fuller's original plan. A film "doctor," David Bretherton,
claimed the film was too violent and had no sympathetic characters. He at-
tempted to reverse these "problems." It is quite likely that the novel version
of the project is much closer to Fuller's original long cut. Among other things,
it is long, violent and has a more objective view of the main characters. The
film, as it stands, contains many great moments, but the book is a masterpiece,

a sustained tour de force that fully captures the epic scope and bloody toll of World War II.

Fuller's battlefields are a surreal landscape of showering blood and cascading body parts. Soldiers are scorched by "grilled entrails," severed heads land in foxholes, eyes still open and staring. Soldiers become "blowtops," go crazy and shoot their own men and are in turn executed by their own sergeant. Fuller can move in close to describe the muscle by muscle agony of a steep rock climb, or sketch in a new character's background in two paragraphs and kill him in the third. Death can come in a moment of explosive oblivion, leaving no trace, or it can come quietly, freezing a body in its last living act, mouth filled with food. No matter how bravely his soldiers fight, Fuller avoids macho posturing, using black comedy to illustrate their constant state of anxiety: A GI carries a stethoscope in the feeble hope someone will use it on him if he is wounded, and not bury him alive, "Y'know, snap judgments by medics." But Fuller can also pull back, like the camera crane he is fond of using in his movies, and capture the size and spectacle of his battle scenes: D-Day, the invasion of Sicily, a dazzling "goum" cavalry charge through the ruins of a Roman coliseum.

The Big Red One, the novel, is the best evidence of what Fuller's four- or six-hour cut of the film must have been like. The novel deserves, however, to stand on its own merits as one of the great firsthand accounts of infantry combat in the literature of World War II.

Quint's World (first published in France as *La Grande Mêlée*) is based on a screenplay written in the 1970s. The script, *Battle Royal*, may have been conceived in the same spirit as *Dead Pigeon on Beethoven Street*, a smaller-scale tale of cynical, watergate-ish intrigue among world leaders in Europe. *Dead Pigeon* was a self-conscious work, with one eye winking at Fuller's cult of auteurs and cinephiles, and *Battle Royal* may have had the same intentions—Fuller planned to cast European film directors as the leaders of their respective countries. *Quint's World*, in any case, is infinitely better than *Dead Pigeon* in either its filmed or novelized incarnations. Briskly cinematic, cleverly plotted and well-written, it is a highly entertaining satire on the international-conspiracy-thriller genre.

Eschewing any attempt at believability, Fuller writes hilariously cynical scenes of back-stabbing summit conferences, with Europe's presidents and prime ministers acting like backroom ward healers. Among Fuller's amusing conceits is the notion of each leader having his own personal hit man, and the variously colorful assassins (including a French ballet dancer) are each given their own murderous set-piece. Quint himself, a seedy bum fresh out of an English insane asylum, must rank as one of the most likable of Fuller's many iconoclastic excuses for a "hero."

Appendix B:
Unrealized Projects

Fuller, like most Hollywood writers and directors, has worked on many scripts and projects that never became finished films. Being an unusually fast and fertile writer, Fuller naturally has had more of these unfilmed stories than the average filmmaker. In some periods he is said to have written a half-dozen finished original screenplays per year. Many of these represent momentary enthusiasms or commercial prospects quickly run up the flagpole for this or that passing producer, written and then forgotten. Others are long-cherished and very personal projects that Fuller has tinkered with and talked about for decades. *The Big Red One* was a "dream" project for over 20 years before it was actually produced. A number of his unfilmed scripts have been turned into novels and published in paperback editions.

What follows is a small selection of these unrealized projects, from the 1940s to the present:

Uncle Sam: An original screenplay sold to RKO, this was apparently a hard-hitting exposé of the Department of Immigration, Senator McCarren, and the exploitation of the postwar immigration situation. Fuller named names, and RKO decided it was a little too hard-hitting.

Saber Tooth: A science fiction adventure story set in the crater of an extinct volcano, this Fox project originated with Philip Dunne. Fuller collaborated with Dunne, then wrote another draft on his own. The film was budgeted and set to go, then dropped at the last minute. Fox had just made *The Robe*, and Zanuck supposedly explained, "And we haven't got any more money left."

Tigrero: A story set in the jungles of Brazil, concerning a rancher and his wife and a *tigrero*, a man who hunts jaguars with a spear. The story touches on Fuller's thematic interest in the nature of heroism and cowardice, with a typically provocative upending of romantic cliché. When the rancher must risk his own life to save his wife's, he doesn't do it, a reaction the tigrero teaches the woman to accept. "Like all human beings, her husband loved her very much but be loved himself a little more." Fuller hoped to shoot the film in the South American wilds, and spent many weeks location-hunting among the tribal warriors and headshrinkers of the Matto Grosso. "They made me guest of honor. And they shrunk a head. It takes three days and three nights. . . . I asked them through an interpreter as a special favor, when they shrink the head, to stop the ceremony at night because I can't photograph at night." Fuller says the studio was behind the film, set to star John Wayne as the tigrero and Tyrone Power as the husband, but the insurance companies refused to insure a production filming on such dangerous locations. Some of the 16mm footage Fuller shot in Brazil turns up in *Shock Corridor*.

Flowers of Evil: The original starting point seems to have been a treatment by Noel Burch and Mark Goodman, a modern adaptation of *Lysistrata* by Aristophanes. Fuller found the material "very bad" but inspiring and wrote an original script, adding a title and epigram ("I have found it amusing to extract beauty from evil") from Baudelaire, and turning the plot into "zany" "semi–science fiction" about a secret society of beautiful women of all nations — the Flowers of Evil — who use violence, science and sex in a plot to stop all wars. The opening scene involves a ballerina pirouetting from the stage to the street as she flees a homicidal all-female motorcycle gang; the final scene is set in outer space with the leading lady abandoned, revolving endlessly into the darkness. "I thought that was a hell of an ending." Two Paris-based American producers hired Fuller to make the picture in 1966. At the last minute one of the producers told him, "'We don't have the money, we never really had it. We thought you would get the money for us'. . . . I hit the ceiling."

The Rifle: Fuller's "Vietnam yarn," which he had hoped to film in 1969 at the height of the war. An old M1 rifle, a World War II "veteran," enters the lives of various quaint characters — a legendary colonel with a death wish, a 14-year-old Vietcong assassin, an insane French nun, a vampiric soldier who steals the blood from the wounded. Fuller planned to shoot the film as an audacious technical experiment, an elaborate, on-location version of Hitchcock's technique for *Rope* — continuous, ten-minute takes, the only cuts being for reel changes. Vietnam war stories were anathema in Hollywood until long after the war ended (with the exception of John Wayne's gung-ho personal production of *The Green Berets*), and Fuller could not find anyone willing to back this ambitious project. If such things can be calculated, then *The Rifle* seems the greatest loss of all the "lost" Fuller movies.

The Eccentrics: Fuller spun this out for a Spanish distributor who had co-produced Welles' *Chimes at Midnight*. Written in Madrid in the summer of 1967 — the "summer of love" — it is Fuller's headlong jump onto the hippie/psychedelia bandwagon. A rich and famous female writer, a combination of Virginia Woolf and George Bernard Shaw, has had a mental breakdown, and gathers a band of hippies — "young, broken-down, weird, eccentric, talented, artistic types" — around her to relax her mind. Fuller saw the film as filled with stream-of-consciousness imagery and dream sequences, as well as assorted beards, beads and Nehru jackets. Jennifer Jones agreed to play the part of the Virginia Woolf—like lead. One month before production in Spain, Jones "couldn't" leave the U.S. and the two producers had a legal tangle. Fuller: "I got fed up and I left."

The Lusty Days: A Civil War story "without a battle and without a death. . . . It's funny, it's light . . . a whole world that people didn't even know existed." Fuller describes an un-solemn Lincoln doing what it takes to get re-elected. "The story of a civilian in war . . . who goes out and gathers the soldiers' votes in the battlefields for the election, and uses a girl's ass, a French girl's ass, to get Lincoln reelected president of the United States."

Balzac: Fuller has been working on a script about the writer's life off and on for over 20 years. It would be a film filled with sexual incident and adventure. The opening scene involves young Balzac and his mother in a runaway stagecoach, hurtling close to a 500-foot drop. The future novelist climbs out of the coach and works his way along the horses, mounts one and saves the day. "If you never heard of Balzac it makes no difference. You'll meet him! And then you'll want to become familiar with this sonofabitch's copy!"

The Charge at San Juan Hill: An action epic about the famous battle of the Spanish-American War, led by future President Teddy Roosevelt. Fuller had actually met a veteran of the battle, the trumpeter who blew the charge, in 1957. "He told me exactly what happened on that hill and it will make one hell of an exciting film, far more exciting than anything dreamed up by pro-paganda salesmen."

Battle Royal: An international thriller, partly inspired by the Watergate scandal, and later turned into a novel. The cynical storyline involves a sleazy conpiracy by several European leaders. Fuller planned to have each leader played by an appropriate European film director—Truffaut as the president of France, Bertolucci the president of Italy, Leni Riefenstahl as the German chancellor (!), and so on. This script became one of the best-written and most entertaining of Fuller's later published novels.

Combat Duty-Paris: One of Fuller's collaborations with his wife, Christa, this is a light-hearted tale of some young American Marines in Paris experiencing romance and culture shock under the tutelage of a French actress.

Bagman: Hardboiled thriller about a "bagman," a man who transports large sums of cash between mobsters and various politicians, world leaders and businesses, and makes the mistake of spending "a couple of bucks." Fuller's story details an alternate world of international money laundering and multi-million dollar cash transactions. The film would open with a bit of poetry about a bagman, ascribed to Al Capone—"I made Capone a poet; I made it up but I give him the credit."

Filmography

Films as Writer-Director

I Shot Jesse James

Lippert Productions (1948)
Filmed in Los Angeles, November 1948.
Running Time: 81 min.
Director: Samuel Fuller
Script: Samuel Fuller
Executive Producer: Robert Lippert
Producer: Carl Hittleman
Director of Photography: Ernest Miller
Editor: Paul Landres
Music: Albert Glasser (Song: Katherine Glasser)
Art Director: Frank Hotaling
Assistant Director: Johnny Grubbs
Camera Operator: Archie Dalzell
Set Decorators: James Redd, John McCarthy
Cast: John Ireland (Bob Ford), Preston Foster (John Kelley), Barbara Britton (Cynthy Waters), Reed Hadley (Jesse James), J. Edward Bromberg (Harry Kane), Tom Tyler (Frank James), Victor Kilian (Soapy), Barbara Woodell (Mrs. Zee James), Tom Noonan (Charles Ford), Byron Foulger (Room Clerk), Eddie Dunn (Bartender), Jeni LeGon (Maid), Phil Pine (Man in Saloon), Robin Short (Troubadour), Margia Dean (Singer in Bar), Gene Collins (Young Man).

The Baron of Arizona

Lippert Productions (1949)
Filmed in Los Angeles, Oct–Nov. 1949.
Running Time: 90 min.
Director: Samuel Fuller
Script: Samuel Fuller
Producer: Carl Hittleman

147

Director of Photography: James Wong Howe
Editor: Arthur Hilton
Music: Paul Dunlap
Art Director: P. Frank Sylos
Special Effects: Ray Mercer, Don Steward
Assistant Director: Frank Fox
Camera Operator: Carl Fetters
Set Decorators: Otto Siegel, Ray Robinson
Costumes: Alfred Berke, Kitty Mayor
Cast: Vincent Price (James Addison Reavis), Ellen Drew (Sofia Peralta-Reavis),
    Beulah Bondi (Lorna Morales), Reed Hadley (John Griff), Vladimir Sokoloff
    (Pepito Alvarez), Robert Barratt (Judge Adams), Robin Short (Lansing), Barbara
    Woodell (Carry Lansing), Tina Rome (Rita), Margia Dean (Marquesa), Edward
    Keane (Surveyor Miller), Gene Roth (Father Guardian), Karen Kester (Sofia as
    Child), Joseph Green, Fred Kohler, Jr., Tristram Coffin, I. Stanford Jolley,
    Terry Frost, Angelo Rosito, Zachery Yaconelli, Adolfo Ornelas, Wheaton
    Chambers, Robert O'Neill, Stephen Harrison, Stuart Holmes, Jonathan Hale.

The Steel Helmet

Lippert Productions (1950)
Filmed in Los Angeles, October 1950.
Running Time: 84 min.
Director: Samuel Fuller
Script: Samuel Fuller
Executive Producer: Robert Lippert
Producer: Samuel Fuller
Associate Producer: William Berke
Director of Photography: Ernest Miller
Editor: Philip Cahn
Music: Paul Dunlap
Art Director: Theobald Holsopple
Special Effects: Ben Southland, Ray Mercer
Assistant Director: John Francis Murphy
Set Decorator: Clarence Steenson
Costumes: Alfred Berke
Cast: Gene Evans (Sergeant Zack), Robert Hutton (Private Bronte), Richard Loo
    (Sergeant Tanaka), Steve Brodie (Lieutenant Driscoll), James Edwards (Cor-
    poral Thompson), William Chun ("Short Round"), Richard Monahan (Private
    Baldy), Harold Fond (The Red), Sid Melton, Neyle Morrow, Lynn Stallmaster.

Fixed Bayonets

Twentieth Century–Fox (1951)
Filmed in Los Angeles, July–Aug. 1951.

Running Time: 92 min.
Director: Samuel Fuller
Script: Samuel Fuller
Producer: Jules Buck
Director of Photography: Lucien Ballard
Editor: Nick DeMaggio
Music: Roy Webb
Musical Director: Lionel Newman
Orchestration: Maurice de Packh
Art Directors: Lyle Wheeler, George Patrick
Sound: Eugene Grossman, Harry M. Leonard
Special Effects: Fred Sersen
Assistant Director: Paul Melmick
Set Decorators: Thomas Little, Fred J. Rhode
Costumes: Charles LeMaire
Technical Adviser: Capt. Raymond Harvey
Cast: Richard Basehart (Corporal Denno), Gene Evans (Sergeant Rock), Michael
    O'Shea (Sergeant Lonergan), Richard Hylton (Private Wheeler), Craig Hill
    (Lieutenant Gibbs), Skip Homeier (Whitey), Henry Kulky (Vogl), Richard
    Monahan (Walowicz), Paul Richards (Ramirez), George Wesley (Griff), Tony
    Kent (Mainotes), Don Orlando (Borcellino), Patrick Fitzgibbon (Paddy), Neyle
    Morrow (Medic), Mel Pogue (Bulchek), George Conrad (Zablocki), David Wolf-
    son, Buddy Thorpe, Al Negbo, Wyott Ordung, Bill Hickman, James Dean.

Park Row

Samuel Fuller Productions/United Artists (1952)
Filmed in Los Angeles, Jan.–Feb. 1952.
Running Time: 83 min.
Director: Samuel Fuller
Script: Samuel Fuller
Producer: Samuel Fuller
Production Supervisor: Sherman A. Harris
Director of Photography: Jack Russell
Editor: Philip Cahn
Music: Paul Dunlap
Art Director: Theobald Holsopple
Sound: Earl Crain, Sr.
Special Effects: Roscoe S. Cline
Assistant Director: Joseph Depew
Set Decorator: Ray Robinson
Costumes: Jack Miller
Script Supervisor: Helen McCaffay
Cast: Gene Evans (Phineas Mitchell), Mary Welch (Charity Hackett), Bela Kovacs
    (Ottmar Mergenthaler), Herbert Heyes (Josiah Davenport), Tina Rome (Jenny
    O'Rourke), George O'Hanlon (Steve Brodie), J. M. Kerrigan (Dan O'Rourke),

Forrest Taylor (Charles Leach), Don Orlando (Mr. Angelo), Neyle Morrow (Thomas Guest), Dick Elliott, Stuart Randall, Dee Pollock, Hal K. Dawson, Charles Horwath.

Pickup on South Street

Twentieth Century-Fox (1953)
Filmed in Los Angeles, Sept.–Oct. 1952.
Running Time: 80 min.
Director: Samuel Fuller
Script: Samuel Fuller (Story credited to Dwight Taylor.)
Producer: Jules Schermer
Director of Photography: Joe MacDonald
Editor: Nick De Maggio
Music: Leigh Harline
Musical Director: Lionel Newman
Orchestration: Edward Powell
Art Directors: Lyle Wheeler, George Patrick
Sound: Winston H. Leverett, Harry M. Leonard
Special Effects: Ray Kellogg
Assistant Director: Ad Schaumer
Set Decorator: Al Orenbach
Costumes: Charles LeMaire Travilla
Cast: Richard Widmark (Skip McCoy), Jean Peters (Candy), Thelma Ritter (Moe Williams), Murvyn Vye (Captain Tiger), Richard Kiley (Joey), Willis Bouchey (Zara), Milburn Stone (Wineki), Henry Slate (MacGregor), Victor Perry (Lightnin' Louie), Jerry O'Sullivan (Enyart), Harry Carter (Dietrich), George E. Stone (Clerk), George Eldredge (Fenton), Stuart Randall (Police Commissioner), Frank Kumagi (Lum), George Berkeley, Emmett Lynn, Maurice Samuels, Parley Baer, Jay Loftlin, Virginia Carroll, Roger Moore.
Winner, Bronze Lion, Venice Film Festival 1953
Remade in South African setting as *Capetown Affair* (1967), directed by Robert D. Webb, starring James Brolin, Jacqueline Bisset and Claire Trevor.

Hell and High Water

Twentieth Century-Fox (1954)
Filmed in Los Angeles, June–Aug. 1953.
Running Time: 103 min.
Director: Samuel Fuller
Script: Jesse L. Lasky, Jr., Samuel Fuller, from a story by David Hempstead
Producer: Raymond A. Klune
Director of Photography: Joe MacDonald (Color, Cinemascope).
Editor: James B. Clark
Music: Alfred Newman (Song lyrics, Harry Powell)

Orchestration: Edward B. Powell
Art Directors: Lyle Wheeler, Leland Fuller
Sound: Eugene Grossman, Roger Heman
Special Effects: Ray Kellogg
Assistant Director: Ad Schaumer
Set Decorators: Walter M. Scott, Stuart Reiss
Costumes: Charles LeMaire, Travilla
Cast: Richard Widmark (Adam Jones), Bella Darvi (Denise Gerard), Cameron
    Mitchell (Brodski), Victor Francen (Professor Montel), Gene Evans (Holter),
    David Wayne (Walker), Richard Loo (Fujimori), Stephen Bekassy (Neuman),
    Wong Artane (Chin Lee), Rollin Moriyama (Joto), William Hip (Ho Sin).

House of Bamboo

Twentieth Century–Fox (1955)
Filmed in Japan, Feb.–March 1955.
Running Time: 102 min.
Director: Samuel Fuller
Script: Harry Kleiner, Samuel Fuller (Storyline based on Kleiner's script for *Street
    with No Name.*)
Producer: Buddy Adler
Director of Photography: Joe MacDonald (Color, Cinemascope)
Editor: James B. Clark
Music: Leigh Harline (Song: Leigh Harline, Jack Brooks)
Musical Director: Lionel Newman
Orchestration: Edward B. Powell
Art Directors: Lyle Wheeler, Addison Hehr
Sound: John D. Stack, Harry M. Leonard
Special Effects: Ray Kellogg
Assistant Director: David Silver
Set Decorators: Walter M. Scott, Stuart Reiss
Costumes: Charles Le Maire
Color Consultant: Leonard Doss
Cast: Robert Stack (Eddie Spanier/Kenner), Robert Ryan (Sandy Dawson),
    Shirley Yamaguchi (Mariko), Cameron Mitchell (Griff), Brad Dexter (Captain
    Hanson), Sessue Hayakawa (Inspector Kita), Biff Elliott (Webber), Sandro
    Giglio (Ceran), Elko Hanabusa (Japanese Screaming Woman), DeForest Kelley
    (Charlie), Peter Gray (Willy), Robert Quarry (Phil), John Doucette, Teru
    Shimada, Robert Hosoi, Jack Maeshiro, May Takasugi, Neyle Morrow, Reiko
    Hayakawa, Sandy Ozeka, the Kokusai Theatre Troupe.

Run of the Arrow

Globe Enterprises/RKO (1957)
(Released by Universal)
Filmed on location in Utah and California, June–July 1956.

Running Time: 86 min.
Director: Samuel Fuller
Script: Samuel Fuller
Producer: Samuel Fuller
Production Manager: Gene Bryant
Director of Photography: Joseph Biroc (Technicolor)
Editor: Gene Fowler, Jr.
Music: Victor Young
Art Directors: Albert D'Agostino, Jack Okey
Sound: Virgil Smith
Assistant Director: Ben Chapman
Set Decorator: Bert Granger
Cast: Rod Steiger (O'Meara), Sarita Montiel (Yellow Moccasin), Brian Keith (Captain Clark), Ralph Meeker (Lieutenant Driscoll), Jay C. Flippen (Walking Coyote), Charles Bronson (Blue Buffalo), Olive Carey (Mrs. O'Meara), Col. Tim McCoy (General Allen), H. M. Wynant (Crazy Wolf), Neyle Morrow (Lieutenant Stockwell), Frank de Kova (Red Cloud), Stuart Randall (Colonel Taylor), Frank Warner, Billy Miller, Chuck Hayward, Carleton Young, Chuck Roberson. (Sarita Montiel's voice dubbed by Angie Dickinson.)

China Gate

Globe Enterprises/Twentieth Century–Fox (1957)
Filmed in Los Angeles, January 1957.
Running Time: 97 min.
Director: Samuel Fuller
Script: Samuel Fuller
Producer: Samuel Fuller
Director of Photography: Joseph Biroc
Editor: Gene Fowler, Jr., Dean Harrison
Music: Victor Young and Max Steiner (Song by Victor Young, Harold Adamson, sung by Nat "King" Cole)
Music Editor: Audrey Granville
Art Director: John Mansbridge
Sound: Jean Speak
Sound Editor: Bert Schoenfield
Special Effects: Norman Breedlove, Linwood Dunn
Assistant Director: Harold E. Knox
Costumes: Henry West, Beau Van den Ecker
Cast: Gene Barry (Brock), Angie Dickinson ("Lucky Legs"), Nat "King" Cole (Goldie), Paul Dubov (Captain Caumont), Lee Van Cleef (Major Cham), George Givot (Corporal Pigalle), Gerald Milton (Private Andreades), Neyle Morrow (Leung), Marcel Dalio (Father Paul), Maurice Marsac (Colonel De Sars), Warren Hsieh (Boy), Paul Busch (Corporal Kruger), Sasha Harden (Private Jazzi), James Hong (Charlie), William Soo Hoo, Weaver Levy, Ziva Rodann.

Forty Guns

Globe Enterprises/Twentieth Century–Fox (1957)
Filmed in Los Angeles, April–May 1957.
Running Time: 80 min.
Director: Samuel Fuller
Script: Samuel Fuller
Producer: Samuel Fuller
Director of Photography: Joseph Biroc
Editor: Gene Fowler, Jr.
Music: Harry Sukman
Songs: "High Ridin' Woman with a Whip" by Harold Adamson, Harry Sukman; "God Has His Arms Around Me" by Harold Adamson and Victor Young.
Art Director: John Mansbridge
Sound: Jean Speak, Harry M. Leonard
Special Effects: Norman Breedlove, L. B. Abbott, Linwood Dunn
Assistant Director: Harold E. Knox
Set Decorators: Walter M. Scott, Chester Bayhi
Costumes: Charles LeMaire, Leah Rhodes
Cast: Barbara Stanwyck (Jessica Drummond), Barry Sullivan (Griff Bonnell), Dean Jagger (Ned Logan), John Ericson (Brock Drummond), Gene Barry (Wes Bonnell), Robert Dix (Chico Bonnell), "Jidge" Carroll (Barney Cashman), Paul Dubov (Judge Macy), Gerald Milton (Shotgun Spanger), Ziva Rodann (Rio), Hand Worden (John Chisum), Sandra Wirth (Chico's Girlfriend), Neyle Morrow (Wiley), Eve Brent (Louvenia Spanger), Chuck Roberson (Swain), Chuck Hayward (Charlie Savage).

Verboten

Globe Enterprises/RKO (1959)
(Released by Columbia)
Filmed in Los Angeles, April–May 1958.
Running Time: 94 min.
Director: Samuel Fuller
Script: Samuel Fuller
Producer: Samuel Fuller
Production Manager: Walter Daniels
Director of Photography: Joseph Biroc
Editor: Philip Cahn
Music: Harry Sukman; Wagner, Beethoven
Art Director: John Mansbridge
Sound: Bert Schoenfeld, Jean Speak
Special Effects: Norman Breedlove
Assistant Director: Gordon McLean
Camera Operator: William Cline
Set Decorator: Glen L. Daniels

Costumes: Berniece Pontrelli, Harry West
Technical Adviser: Commander Raymond Harvey
Cast: James Best (Sgt. David Brent), Susan Cummings (Helga Schiller), Tom Pittman (Bruno Eckart), Paul Dubov (Captain Harvey), Harold Daye (Franz), Dick Kallman (Helmuth), Stuart Randall (Colonel), Steven Geray (Burgermeister), Anna Hope (Frau Schiller), Robert Boon (SS Officer), Neyle Morrow (Sergeant Kellogg), Sasha Harden (Erich), Paul Busch (Guenther), Joseph Turkel, Charles Horvath, Sam Fuller (voiceovers)

The Crimson Kimono

Globe Enterprises/Columbia (1959)
Filmed in Los Angeles, Feb.–March 1959.
Running Time: 82 min.
Director: Samuel Fuller
Script: Samuel Fuller
Producer: Samuel Fuller
Director of Photography: Sam Leavitt
Editor: Jerome Thoms
Music: Harry Sukman
Orchestration: Jack Hayves, Leo Shuken
Art Directors: William E. Flannery, Robert Boyle
Sound: Josh Westmoreland
Sound Recording Supervisor: John Livadry
Assistant Director: Floyd Joyer
Set Decorator: James Crowe
Costumes: Bernice Pontrelli
Cast: Glenn Corbett (Det. Charlie Bancroft), James Shigeta (Det. Joe Kojaku), Victoria Shaw (Christine Downes), Anna Lee (Mac), Paul Dubov (Casale), Jaclynne Greene (Roma Wilson), Neyle Morrow (Hansel), Gloria Pall (Sugar Torch), Barbara Hayden (Mother), George Yoshinaga (Willy Hidaka), Kaye Elhardt (Nun), Aya Oyama, George Koamura, Ryosho S. Sogabe, Robert Okazaki, Fuji, Walter Burke, Sam Fuller (voiceovers).

Underworld USA

Globe Enterprises/Columbia (1960)
Filmed in Los Angeles, July–Aug. 1960.
Running Time: 99 min.
Director: Samuel Fuller
Script: Samuel Fuller (title from articles by Joseph F. Dineen)
Producer: Samuel Fuller
Director of Photography: Hal Mohr
Editor: Jerome Thomas
Music: Harry Sukman

Art Director: Robert Peterson
Sound: Charles J. Rice
Sound Supervisor: Josh Westmoreland
Assistant Director: Floyd Joyer
Set Decorator: Bill Calvert
Costumes: Bernice Pontrelli
Cast: Cliff Robertson (Tolly Devlin), Beatrice Kay (Sandy), Larry Gates (Driscoll),
    Richard Rust (Gus), Dolores Dorn (Cuddles), Robert Emhardt (Connors), Paul
    Dubov (Gela), Gerald Milton (Gunther), Allan Greuner (Smith), David Kent
    (Young Tolly), Neyle Morrow (Barney), Henry Norell, Sally Mills, Tina Rome,
    Robert Lieb, Peter Brocco.

Merrill's Marauders

United States Productions/Warner Bros. (1962)
Filmed in the Philippines, March–May 1961.
Running Time: 98 min.
Director: Samuel Fuller
Script: Samuel Fuller, Milton Sperling, from book by Charlton Ogburn, Jr.
Producer: Milton Sperling
Production Supervisor: William Magginetti
Director of Photography: William Clothier
Editor: Folmar Blangsted
Music: Howard Jackson
Art Director: William Magginetti
Sound: Francis M. Stahl
Special Effects: Ralph Ayres
Assistant Director: William Kissel
Technical Adviser: Lt.-Colonel Samuel Wilson
Cast: Jeff Chandler (Brig.-General Frank Merrill), Ty Hardin (Lt. Lee Stockton),
    Peter Brown (Bullseye), Andrew Duggan (Major Nemeny), Will Hutchins
    (Chowhound), Claude Akins (Sgt. Kolowicz), Charles Briggs (Muley), Chuck
    Roberson, Chuck Hayward, Jack C. Williams, Chuck Hicks, Vaughan Wilson,
    Pancho Magolona.

Shock Corridor

Fromkess-Firks/Allied Artists (1963)
Filmed in Los Angeles, Feb.–March 1963.
Running Time: 101 min.
Director: Samuel Fuller
Script: Samuel Fuller
Producer: Samuel Fuller
Production Manager: Herbert G. Luft
Director of Photography: Stanley Cortez (Hallucinations shot by Fuller in Japan
    and Brazil.)

Editor: Jerome Thoms
Music: Paul Dunlap
Art Director: Eugene Lourie
Sound: Phil Mitchel
Special Effects: Linwood Dunn
Assistant Director: Floyd Joyer
Set Decorator: Charles Thompson
Costumes: Einar H. Bourman
Choreography: John Gregory
Cast: Peter Breck (Johnny Barrett), Constance Towers (Cathy), Gene Evans
    (Boden), James Best (Stuart), Hari Rhodes (Trent), Larry Tucker (Pagliacci),
    Philip Ahn (Dr. Fong), William Zuckert (Swanee), John Mathews (Dr. Cristo),
    Neyle Morrow (Psycho), Rachel Romen, Marie Devereux (Nymphos), John
    Craig, Frankie Gerstle, Paul Dubov, Lucille Curtis, Karen Conrad, Barbara
    Perry, Marlene Manners, Jeanette Dana, Allison Daniell, Chuck Hicks, Ray
    Baxter, Linda Barrett, Harry Fleer.

The Naked Kiss

Fromkess-Firks/Allied Artists (1964)
Filmed in Los Angeles, Oct.–Nov. 1963.
Running Time: 93 min.
Director: Samuel Fuller
Script: Samuel Fuller
Producer: Samuel Fuller
Executive Producers: Leo Fromkess, Sam Firks
Director of Photography: Stanley Cortez
Editor: Jerome Thoms
Music: Paul Dunlap
Art Director: Eugene Lourie
Sound: Alfred J. Overton
Assistant Director: Nate Levinson
Camera Operator: Frank Dugas
Set Decorator: Victor Gangelin
Costumes: Einar H. Bourman, Act III
Cast: Constance Towers (Kelly), Anthony Eisley (Griff), Michael Dante (Grant),
    Virginia Grey (Candy), Patsy Kelly (Mac), Betty Bronson (Miss Josephine),
    Marie Devereux (Buff), Karen Conrad (Dusty), Linda Francis (Rembrandt),
    Barbara Perry (Edna), Betty Robinson (Bunny), Christopher Barry (Peanuts),
    Walter Mathews (Mike), George Spell (Tim), Gerald Michenaud (Kip), Patty
    Robinson (Angel Face), Neyle Morrow (Officer Sam), Monte Mansfield (Far-
    lunde), Fletcher Fist (Barney), Gerald Milton (Zookie), Edy Williams (Hatrack),
    Sally Mills (Marshmallow), Breena Howard, Michael Barrere, Patricia Gayle,
    Sheila Mintz, Bill Sampson.

Shark

Heritage Enterprises (1969)
Filmed in Mexico, 1967.
Running Time: 92 min.
Director: Samuel Fuller
Script: Samuel Fuller and John Kingsbridge (from the novel, *His Bones Are Coral* by Victor Canning)
Producers: Jose Luis Calderon; Skip Steloff and Mark Cooper
In Charge of Production: Norman Baer
Post-Production Supervisor: Herbert L. Strock
Director of Photography: Raul Martinez Solares
Second Unit Photography: Said Karen
Editor: Carlos Savage
Music: Rafael Moroyoqui
Art Director: Manuel Fontanals
Cast: Burt Reynolds (Caine), Arthur Kennedy ("Doc"), Barry Sullivan (Professor Mallare), Silvia Pinal (Anna), Carlos Barry ("Runt"), Enrique Lucero (Police Inspector Barok), Manuel Alvarado, Francisco Reyguera, Emilia Stuart.
(Fuller has disowned the film, which was taken out of his hands.)

Dead Pigeon on Beethoven Street

Barvaria Atelier Gesellschaft (1972)
Filmed in Germany, 1971.
Running Time: 102 min.
Director: Samuel Fuller
Script: Samuel Fuller
Director of Photography: Jerzy Lipman
Editor: Liesgret Schmitt-Klink
Art Director: Lothar Kirchem
Cast: Glenn Corbett (Sandy), Christa Lang (Christa), Anton Diffring (Mensur), Eric P. Caspar (Charlie Umlaut), Sieghardt Rupp (Kessin), Alex D'Arcy (Novka), Anthony Ching (Fong), Stephane Audran.

The Big Red One

Lorimar (1980)
Filmed in Israel and Ireland, 1979.
Running Time: 113 min.
Director: Samuel Fuller
Script: Samuel Fuller
Producer: Gene Corman
Director of Photography: Adam Greenberg
Editors: David Bretherton, Morton Tubor

Music: Dana Kaproff
Music Supervision: Bodie Chandler
Art Director: Peter Jamison
Special Effects: Kit West, Peter Dawson, Jeff Clifford
Assistant Director: Arne L. Schmidt
2nd Assistant Director: Todd Corman
Unit Production Manager: Peter Cornberg
2nd Unit Director: Lewis Teague
Gunsmith: Alan Weisman
Cast: Lee Marvin (The Sergeant), Mark Hamill (Griff), Robert Carradine (Zab),
    Bobby DeCicco (Vinci), Kelly Ward (Johnson), Stephane Audran (Walloon),
    Siegfried Rauch (Schroeder), Serge Marquand (Rensonnet), Charles Macauley
    (General/Captain), Alain Doutey (Brohan), Maurice Marsac (Vichy Colonel),
    Colin Gilbert (Dog Face POW), Joseph Clark, Ken Campbell, Doug Werner,
    Perry Lang, Howard Belman, Marthe Villalonga, Giovanna Galetti, Gregori
    Biumistre, Shimon Barre, Mattes Zoffoli, Avraham Ronai, Galit Rotman.

White Dog

Paramount (1982)
Filmed in Los Angeles, 1981.
Running Time: 90 min.
Director: Samuel Fuller
Script: Samuel Fuller, Curtis Hanson (From the novella by Romain Gary.)
Producer: Jon Davison
Director of Photography: Bruce Surtees
Editor: Bernard Gribble
Music: Ennio Morricone
Associate Producer: Richard Hashimoto
Production Designer: Brian Eatwell
Assistant Director: William Scott
2nd Assistant Director: Daniel Attias
Set Decorator: Barbara Krieger
Women's Costumer: Gail Viola
Men's Costumer: Ellis Cohen
Stunt Coordinator: Bob Minor
Dog Trainers: Karl Lewis Miller, Animal Action
Cast: Kristy McNichol (Julie Sawyer), Paul Winfield (Keys), Burl Ives (Carruthers),
    Jameson Parker (Roland Gray), Marshall Thompson (Director), Martine Daw-
    son (Martine), Paul Bartel (Cameraman), Neyle Morrow (Soundman), Parley
    Baer (Wilbur Hull), Samuel Fuller (Charlie Felton), Karl Lewis Miller (At-
    tacker), Christa Lang (Nurse), Vernon Weddle (Vet), Helen J. Siff (Pound
    Operator), Glen Garner (Pound Worker), Tony Brubaker (Sweeper driver),
    Hubert Wells (Trainer), Sam Laws (Charlie), Cliff Fellow (Sheriff), Dick Miller,
    Robert Ritchie (Animal trainers), Bob Minor (Joe), Samantha Fuller (Helen),
    Jamie Crowe (Theona), Folsom, Hans, Son, Buster, Duke (Dogs).

Les Voleurs de la nuit/Thieves After Dark

Parafrance Films (1982)
Filmed in France, 1982.
Running Time: 92 min.
Director: Samuel Fuller
Script: Samuel Fuller and Oliver Beer (from Beer's novel, *Le Chant des Enfants Morts*).
Producer: Michel Gue
Director of Photography: Philippe Rousselot
Editor: Catherine Kelber
Music: Ennio Morricone
Art Director: Dominique Andre
Cast: Veronique Jannot (Isabelle), Bobby Di Cicco (Francois), Victor Lanoux (Inspector), Stephan Audran (Isabelle's Mother), Claude Chabrol (Louis Crepin), Camille de Casabianca (Corinne Desterne), Andreas Voutsinas (Jose), Micheline Presle (Morell), Sam Fuller (Zoltan).

Street of No Return

Thunder Films Intl./FR 3 Films Prod./Animatografo/Instituto Portugues de Cinema (1989)
Filmed in Lisbon, Portugal, 1988.
Running Time: 90 min.
Director: Samuel Fuller
Script: Samuel Fuller, Jacques Bral (from the novel of the same name by David Goodis).
Producer: Jacques Bral
Executive Producers: Jacques-Eric Strauss, Patrick Delauneax, Antonio da Cunha Telles
Director of Photography: Pierre-William Glenn
Music: Karl-Heinz Schafer (title song lyrics by Sam Fuller, music by Keith Carradine)
Art Director: Geoffrey Larcher
Cast: Keith Carradine (Michael), Valentina Vargas (Celia), Bill Duke (Borel), Andrea Ferreol (Rhoda), Bernard Fresson (Morin), Marc de Jonge (Eddie), Rebecca Potok (Bertha), Jacques Martial (Gerard), Sergio Godinho (Pernoy), Antonio Rosario (Meathead), Dominique Hulin (Dablin), Gordon Heath (Black Tramp), Joe Abdo (White Tramp), Trevor Stephens (Lambert), Filipe Ferrer (Gauvreau), Jeremy Boultbee (Doctor), Guilherme Filipe (Policeman), Pedro Nunes (Policeman), Christa Lang (Nurse), Samantha Fuller (Young Fan), Joaquim Miranda (Police Officer), Luis Norton De Matos (Police Officer), Samuel Fuller (Chief of Police).

Screen Stories and Screenplays

Hats Off

Grand National (1937)
Running Time: 65 min.
Director: Boris Petroff
Script: Sam Fuller, Edmund Joseph
Producer: Boris Petroff
Director of Photography: Harry Newman
Music: Paul Mertz, songs by Herb Magidson, Ben Oakland
Cast: John Payne (Jimmy Maxwell), Mae Clarke (Jo Allen), Helen Lynd (Ginger
   Connolly), Luis Alberni (Rosero), Skeets Gallagher (Buzz), Franklin Pangborn
   (Churchill), Robert Middlemass (Tex Connolly), George Irving (J. D. Murdoch),
   Clarence Wilson (C. D. Pottingham), Val Stanton, Ernie Stanton (The Two
   Stooges), Jimmy Hollywood, R. D. Bartell, Henry Taylor (The Three Radio
   Rogues).

It Happened in Hollywood

Columbia (1937)
Running Time: 67 min.
Director: Harry Lachman
Script: Sam Fuller, Ethel Hill, Harvey Ferguson (Story by Myles Connolly.)
Director of Photography: Joseph Walker
Editor: Al Clark
Cast: Richard Dix (Tim Bart), Fay Wray (Gloria Gay), Franklin Pangborn (Mr.
   Forsythe), Victor Kilian (Slim), Charlie Arnt (Jed Reed), Granville Bates (Sam
   Bennett), William B. Davidson (Al Howard), Arthur Loft (Pete), Edgar Dearing
   (Stevens), James Donlan (Shorty), Billy Burrud (????), Zelfie Tilbury (Miss Gor-
   don), Harold Goodwin (Buck), Charles Brinley (Pappy).

Gangs of New York

Republic (1938)
Running Time: 67 min.
Director: James Cruze
Script: Wellyn Totman, Sam Fuller, Jack Townley, Charles Francis Royal (Story
   by Sam Fuller, inspired by the book of the same name by Herbert Asbury.)
Producer: Armand Schaefer
Director of Photography: Ernest Miller
Editor: William Morgan
Art Director: John V. Mackay
Cast: Charles Bickford (Rocky/John Franklin), Ann Dvorak (Connie), Alan Baxter

(Dancer), Wynne Gibson (Orchid), Harold Huber (Panatella), Maxie Rosenbloom (Tombstone), Willard Robertson (Sullivan), Charles Trowbridge (Attorney), John Wray (Maddock), Jonathan Hale (Warden), Fred Kohler (Kruger), Howard Phillips (Al Benson), Robert Gleckler (Nolan), Elliot Sullivan (Hopkins), Maurice Cass (Phillips).

Adventure in the Sahara

Columbia (1938)
Running Time: 60 min.
Director: D. Ross Lederman
Script: Maxwell Shane (Story by Sam Fuller.)
Director of Photography: Frank Planer
Editor: Otto Meyer
Cast: Paul Kelly (Jim Wilson), C. Henry Gordon (Captain Savatt), Lorna Gray (Carla Preston), Robert Fiske (Lt. Dumond), Marc Lawrence (Poule), Stanley Brown (Rene Malreau), Dick Curtis, Alan Bridge, Raphael Bennett, Charles Moore, Dwight Frye, Stanley Andrews.

Federal Manhunt

Republic (1939)
Director: Nick Grinde
Script: Maxwell Shane (Story by Sam Fuller, William Lively.)
Producer: Armand Schaefer
Director of Photography: Ernest Miller
Editor: Murray Seldeen
Cast: Robert Livingston (Bill), June Travis (Anne), John Gallaudet (Rennick), Ben Welden (Goldie), Horace MacMahon (Soapy), Charles Halton (Lauber), Gene Morgan (Hawlings), Matt McHugh (Kilgore), Sybil Harris (Mrs. Banning), Jerry Tucker (Scoop), Margaret Mann (Mrs. Ganter), Frank Conklin (Beeber).

Bowery Boy

Republic (1940)
Running Time: 71 min.
Director: William Morgan
Script: Robert Chapin, Harry Kronman, Eugene Solow (Story by Sam Fuller, Sidney Sutherland.)
Producer: Armand Schaefer
Director of Photography: Ernest Miller
Editor: Edward Mann
Music: Cy Feuer
Cast: Dennis O'Keefe (Tom O'Hara), Louise Campbell (Anne Cleary), Jimmy

Lydon (Sock Dolan), Helen Vinson (Peggy Winters), Roger Pryor (J. L. Mason), Paul Hurst (Blubber), Edward Gargan (Hansen), Selmer Jackson (Dr. Crane), John Kelly (Battler), Howard Hickman (Dr. Axel Winters), Frederick Burton (Dr. George Winters), Jack Carr (Flops).

Confirm or Deny

Twentieth Century–Fox (1941)
Running Time: 73 min.
Director: Archie Mayo (replaced Fritz Lang)
Script: Jo Swerling (Story by Samuel Fuller, Henry Wales.)
Producer: Len Hammond
Director of Photography: Leon Shamroy
Editor: Robert Bischoff
Cast: Don Ameche (Mitch), Joan Bennett (Jennifer Carson), Roddy McDowell (Albert Perkins), John Loder (Capt. Channing), Raymond Walburn (Cyrus Sturtevant), Arthur Shields (Jeff), Eric Blore (Mr. Hobbs), Helen Reynolds (Dorothy), Claude Allister (Williams), Roseanne Murray, Stuart Robertson, Queenie Leonard, Jean Prescott, Billy Bevan, Alan Napier, Lumsden Hare, Dennis Hoey, Leonard Carey.

Power of the Press

Columbia (1943)
Running Time: 64 min.
Director: Lew Landers
Script: Robert D. Andrews (From story by Sam Fuller.)
Producer: Leon Barsha
Director of Photography: John Stumar
Editor: Mel Thorsen
Art Director: Lionel Banks
Cast: Guy Kibbee (Ulysses Bradford), Gloria Dickson (Edwina Stephens), Lee Tracy (Griff), Otto Kruger (Howard Rankin), Victor Jory (Oscar Trent), Larry Parks (Jerry Purvis), Rex Williams (Chris Barker), Frank Sully (Mack Gibson), Don Beddoe (Pringle), Douglas Leavitt (Whiffle), Minor Watson (John Carter).

Gangs of the Waterfront

Republic (1945)
Running Time: 55 min.
Director: George Blair
Script: Albert Beich (Story by Sam Fuller.)
Producer: George Blair
Director of Photography: Marcel Le Picard

Editor: Fred Allen
Music: Richard Cherwin
Cast: Robert Armstrong (Dutch Malone/Peter Winkly), Stephanie Bachelor (Jane Rodgers), Martin Kosleck (Anjo Ferranti), Marian Martin (Rita), William Forrest (District Attorney), Wilton Graff (Commissioner Hogan), Eddie Hall, Jack O'Shea, Davison Clark, Dick Elliott.

Shockproof

Columbia (1949)
Running Time: 79 min.
Director: Douglas Sirk
Script: Helen Deutsch, Samuel Fuller
Producer: Helen Deutsch, S. Sylvan Simon
Director of Photography: Charles Lawton, Jr.
Editor: Gene Havlick
Music: George Duning
Art Director: Carl Anderson
Set Decorator: Louis Diage
Costumes: Jean Louis
Cast: Cornel Wilde (Griff Marat), Patricia Knight (Jenny Marsh), John Baragrey (Harry Wesson), Esther Minciotti (Mrs. Marat), Howard St. John (Sam Brooks), Russell Collins (Frederick Bauer), Charles Bates (Tommy Marat), Gilbert Barnett (Barry), Frank Jaquet (Monte), Ann Shoemaker (Dr. Daniels), King Donovan (Joe Wilson), Claire Carleton (Florie), Al Eben (Joe Kobiski), Fred Sears, Jimmy Lloyd, Isabel Withers, Virginia Farmer, Charles Jordan, Buddy Swan, Crane Whitley, Robert R. Stephenson, Richard Benedict, Cliff Clark, Arthur Space, Charles Marsh.

The Tanks Are Coming

Warner Bros. (1951)
Running Time: 90 min.
Director: Lewis Seiler, D. Ross Lederman
Script: Robert Hardy Andrews (Story by Samuel Fuller.)
Producer: Bryan Foy
Director of Photography: Edwin DuPar, Warren Lynch
Editor: James C. Moore
Music: William Lava
Art Director: Leo K. Kuter
Cast: Steve Cochran (Sully), Philip Carey (Rawson), Mari Aldon (Patricia Kane), Paul Picerni (Danny), Harry Bellaver (Lemchek), James Dobson (Ike), George O'Hanlon (Tucker), John McGuire (Col. Matthews), Robert Boon (Heinie), Michael Steele (Sgt. Joe Davis).

Scandal Sheet

Columbia/Edward Small (1952)
Running Time: 82 min.
Director: Phil Karlson
Script: Ted Sherdeman, Eugene Ling and James Poe (From the novel, *The Dark Page* by Samuel Fuller.)
Producer: Edward Small
Director of Photography: Burnett Guffey
Editor: Jerome Thoms
Music: George Duning
Art Director: Robert Peterson
Assistant Director: Frederick Briskin
Cast: John Derek (Steve McCleary), Donna Reed (Julie Allison), Broderick Crawford (Mark Chapman), Rosemary DeCamp (Charlotte Grant), Henry O'Neill (Charlie Barnes), Henry Morgan (Biddle), James Millican (Lt. Davis), Griff Barnett (Judge Hacker), Jonathan Hale (Frank Madison), Ida Moore (Needle Nellie), Perre Watkin, Ralph Reed, Luther Crockett, Charles Cane, Jay Adler.

The Command

Warner Bros. (1954)
Running Time: 94 min.
Director: David Butler
Script: Russell Hughes, Samuel Fuller (From the novel *Rear Guard* by James Warner Bellah.)
Producer: David Weisbart
Director of Photography: Wilfrid M. Cline
Editor: Irene Morra
Music: Dimitri Tiomkin
Cast: Guy Madison (Capt. MacClaw), Joan Weldon (Martha), James Whitmore (Sgt. Elliott), Carl Benton Reid (Col. Janeway), Harvey Lembeck (Gottschalk), Ray Teal (Dr. Trent), Bob Nichols (O'Hirons), Don Shelton (Major Gibbs), Gregg Barton (Capt. Forsythe), Boyd "Red" Morgan (Cpl. Fleming), Zachary Yaconelli (Pellegrini), Renata Vanni (Mrs. Pellegrini), Tom Monroe (Nikirk).

The Deadly Trackers

Cine Film (1973)
Running Time: 105 min.
Director: Barry Shear
Script: Lukas Heller, Sam Fuller (uncredited)
Producer: Fouad Said
Director of Photography: Gabriel Tomes
Cast: Richard Harris (Kilpatrick), Rod Taylor (Brand), Al Lettieri (Gutierrez),

Neville Brand (Choo Choo), William Smith (Schoolboy), Paul Benjamin (Jacob), Pedro Armendariz, Jr. (Blacksmith), Isela Vega (Maria), Kelly Jean Peters (Katherine).

The project began with Fuller as writer-director, but he was removed after irreconcilable differences with Harris. One million dollars worth of footage had been shot and was scrapped.

The Klansman

Paramount (1974)
Running Time: 112 min.
Director: Terence Young
Script: Millard Kaufman, Samuel Fuller (From novel by William Bradford Huie.)
Producer: William Alexander
Director of Photography: Lloyd Ahern
Editor: Gene Milford
Music: Dale O. Warren
Production Designer: John S. Poplin
Cast: Lee Marvin (Sheriff Bascomb), Richard Burton (Breck Stancill), Cameron Mitchell (Deputy Butt Cut Bates), Lola Falana (Loretta Sykes), Lucianna Paluzzi (Trixie), David Huddleston (Mayor Hardy), Linda Evans (Nancy Poteet), O. J. Simpson (Garth), Spence Wil-Dee (Willy Washington), Hoke Howell (Bobby Poteet), Eve Christopher, Ed Call, Morgan Upton, Charles Briggs, Robert Porter, Gary Catus, Wendell Wellman, John Alderson, David Ladd, Virgil Fry, Jeannie Bell, Jo Ann Cowell, Scott E. Lane.

Fuller was originally set to direct but left the project.

Let's Get Harry

Tri-Star (1986)
Running Time: 100 min.
Director: Alan Smithee (Director Stuart Rosenberg had his name removed; Smithee is a traditional pseudonym for dissatisfied Directors Guild members.)
Script: Charles Robert Carner (Story by Mark Feldberg, Samuel Fuller.)
Director of Photography: James A. Contner
Editors: Ralph E. Winters, Rick R. Sparr, Robert Hyams
Music: Brad Fiedel
Cast: Gary Busey (Jack), Robert Duvall (Shrike), Mark Harmon (Harry), Michael Schoeffling (Corey), Tom Wilson (Pachowski), Glenn Frey (Spence), Jerry Hardin (Dean Reilly), Cecile Callan (Theresa), Elpidia Carrillo (Veronica), Rodolfo De Alexandre (Pablo), Ben Johnson (Mr. Burck, Sr.), Bruce Gray (Ambassador Douglas), Gregory Sierra (Alphonso).

Television

The Virginian (1962)

Episode: "It Tolls for Thee"
Running Time: 90 min., with commercials
Director: Samuel Fuller
Script: Samuel Fuller
Producer: Charles Marquis Warren
Director of Photography: Lionel Lindon
Cast: Lee Marvin (Martin Kalig), Lee J. Cobb (Judge Garth), James Drury (The
  Virginian), Doug McClure (Trampas), Gary Clarke (Steve), Pippa Scott (Molly),
  Roberta Shaw (Betsy), Albert Salmi (Quinn), Ron Sobie (Mungo), Warren Kem-
  merling (Sharkey), Michael Mikler (Cord), Jan Stine (Eddie), Duane Grey
  (Jaeger), K. L. Smith (Husky Rider), Francis de Sales (Banker), Brendan Dillon
  (Mr. Bemis), Sidney Smith (Drummond), Stuart Nisbet (Nelson), John Zar-
  emba (Stone).

The Dick Powell Reynolds Aluminum Show (1962)

Episode: 330 Independence S.W.
Running Time: 60 min., with commercials
Director: Samuel Fuller
Script: Allan Sloane
Executive Producer: Dick Powell
Producer: E. J. Rosenberg
Director of Photography: George E. Diskant
Music: Herschel Burke Gilbert
Cast: William Bendix ("Guts" Finney), David McLean (Jim Cochran), Julia Adams
  (Robin), Alan Reed, Jr. (Guy Vista), Yale Summers (Jeff), Ed Kemmer (Mac), Les
  Damon (Mr. Somers), Adrienne Ellis (Connie), Norman Alden (Gooby),
  Michael Harvey (Bill), Bert Freed (Joe Vista).
Unsold pilot for a series on the adventures of a two-fisted troubleshooter for the
  Department of Health, Education & Welfare.

Iron Horse (1966)

ABC TV
Episode 4: "The Man from New Chicago"
Running Time: 60 min., with commercials
Director: Samuel Fuller
Script: Mort R. Lewis
Executive Producer: Charles Marquis Warren
Producer: Stephen Kandel

Director of Photography: Fred Jackman
Music: Dominic Frontiere
Cast: Dale Robertson (Ben Calhoun), Gary Collins (Dave Tarrant), Bob Random (Barnabus Rogers), Duane Grey (Reno), Sy Prescott (Aces), Anthony Brand (Clay), Jim Shepard (Boaz), Tom Steele (Miner), James Anderson (Nations), John Milford (Johnny Spanish), Madlyn Rhue (Angela).

Iron Horse (1966)

ABC TV
Episode 10: "High Devil"
Running Time: 60 min., with commercials
Director: Samuel Fuller
Script: Samuel Fuller
Executive Producer: Charles Marquis Warren
Producer: Stephen Kandel
Director of Photography: Fred Jackman
Music: Dominic Frontiere
Cast: Dale Robertson, Gary Collins, Bob Random, James Best (Chico), Louise Sorel (Jez), Charles Grey (Red Vitel), Hardie Albright (Mr. Wilson), Dal Jenkins (Razor Joe), George Winters (Telegram Boy), Fred Dale, G. D. Spradling.

Iron Horse (1966)

ABC TV
Episode 17: "Volcano Wagon"
Running Time: 60 min., with commercials
Director: Samuel Fuller
Script: Ken Trevey
Executive Producer: Charles Marquis Warren
Producer: Stephen Kandel
Cast: Dale Robertson, Gary Collins, Bob Random, Roger Torrey (Nils Torvald).

Iron Horse (1966)

ABC TV
Episode 20: "Hellcat"
Running Time: 60 min., with commercials
Director: Samuel Fuller
Script: Samuel Fuller and Oliver Crawford
Executive Producer: Charles Marquis Warren
Producer: Stephen Kandel
Cast: Dale Robertson, Harry Landers (Yancey), Vincent Beck (Lanker), Noshima (Noshima).

Iron Horse (1966)

ABC TV
Episode 21: "Banner with a Strange Device"
Running Time: 60 min., with commercials
Director: Samuel Fuller
Script: John O'Dea and Arthur Rowe
Executive Producer: Charles Marquis Warren
Producer: Stephen Kandel
Cast: Dale Robertson, Bob Random (Barnabas Rogers and Jeff Clayborne), Roger
    Torrey (Nils Torvald), Tony Young (Tower), Robert B. Williams (Store-keeper).

The work on both *The Virginian* and *Iron Horse* came about through Fuller's
friendship with producer Charles Marquis Warren.
    In addition, Fuller directed the pilot episode for an unsold television series,
Dogface. The proposed series would have been an anthology of true stories about
American soldiers.

On Screen Appearances

1955: *House of Bamboo,* directed by Fuller. Cameo as policeman.
1964: *Pierrot le Fou,* directed by Jean-Luc Godard. Cameo, as himself at party.
1966: *Brigitte et Brigitte,* directed by Luc Moullet. Plays himself.
1970: *The Last Movie,* directed by Dennis Hopper. Small role as Hollywood
    director of "Peruvian Western."
1973: *Dead Pigeon on Beethoven Street,* directed by Fuller. Cameo, during
    credits.
1973: *The Young Nurses,* directed by Clinton Kimbrough. Cameo.
1977: *Der Amerikanische Freund/The American Friend,* directed by Wim Wen-
    ders. Plays Mobster-Porno Producer.
1977: *Scott Joplin,* directed by Jeremy Paul Kagan. Cameo.
1979: *1941,* directed by Steven Spielberg. Cameo as Army officer.
1982: *Der Stand der Dinge/The State of Things,* directed by Wim Wenders. Plays
    veteran cinematographer.
1982: *White Dog,* directed by Fuller. Plays Charlie Felton.
1983: *Hammett,* directed by Wim Wenders. Cameo in pool hall.
1984: *Slapstick,* directed by Steven Paul. Plays Col. Sharp.
1984: *Les Voleurs de la nuit/Thieves After Dark,* directed by Fuller. Plays Zoltan.
1987: *Fuller: Frame by Frame,* directed by Andre Labarthe. Documentary short
    with Fuller analyzing the opening of *Pickup on South Street.*
1987: *Helsinki Napoli All Night Long,* directed by Mika Kaurismaki. Featured
    role as comical gangster.
1988: *Return to Salem's Lot,* directed by Larry Cohen. Featured role as gun-
    toting vampire hunter.
1988: *Falkenau: The Impossible,* documentary directed by Emil Weiss, using

Fuller's 16mm footage of activities at Falkenau concentration camp after its liberation by U.S. Army. New footage features Fuller on camera as commentator and returning to the area of the camp.

1989: *Sons,* directed by Alexandre Rockwell. Fuller plays paralyzed New Jersey father, taken on last trip to Paris and Normandy by his three sons.

1989: *Street of No Return,* directed by Fuller. Plays Chief of Police (voice and shadow only).

1990: *Hollywood Mavericks,* A.F.I. documentary, contains footage of Fuller interviewed at a Colorado film festival.

Selected Bibliography

Books

Amiel, Olivier. *Samuel Fuller.* Paris: Henri Veyrier, 1985.

Garnham, Nicholas. *Samuel Fuller.* New York: Viking, 1971.

Guerif, François. *Sans Espoir de Retour.* Paris: Henri Veyrier, 1989.

Hardy, Phil. *Sam Fuller.* New York: Praeger, 1970.

Narboni, Jean, and Noel Simsolo. *Il Etait Une Fois . . . Samuel Fuller.* Paris: 1986.

Interviews

Bjorkman, Stig and Mark Shivas. "Samuel Fuller: Two Interviews, Paris 1965 and California 1969," *Movie* 17 (Winter 1969-70).

Blumenfeld, Samuel and Serge Kaganski. "*Les Cigares du Pharaon,*" *Les Inrockuptibles* July/Aug. 1991).

Christie, Ian Leslie, Garnham, Nicholas, and others. "Samuel Fuller, a Cinema Interview," *Cinema* Number 5 (February 1970).

Fisher, William. "The Wham of Sam," *Passion* Issue 51 (1986).

Sherman, Eric and Martin Rubin. *The Director's Event.* New York: Atheneum, 1970.

Thompson, Richard. "The Flavor of Ketchup," *Film Comment,* (Jan.-Feb. 1977).

Wiener, R. M. M. "Ex-Soldier Fuller's Dreams Realized in 'Big Red One,'" *Boxoffice* (July 21, 1980).

Articles

Ansen, David. "An Unblinking View of War," *Newsweek,* July 28, 1980.

Blume, Mary. "Samuel Fuller – 'B' Director or Genius?" *The Los Angeles Times,* November 30, 1974.

Canham, Kingsley. "The World of Samuel Fuller," *Film* Number 55 (Summer 1969).

Cook, Bruce. "Sam Fuller Lands with 'The Big Red One,'" *American Film,* June 1979.

"Daisies from the Killing Ground," *Newsweek,* May 28, 1984.
Godard, Jean-Luc. "Forty Guns," *Cahiers du Cinéma* 76 (November 1957).
Hoberman, J. "Sam Fuller: Gate Crasher at the Auteur Limits," *The Village Voice,* July 2–8, 1980.
Jacobson, Mark. "This Gun for Hire," *The Village Voice,* August 30, 1976.
McCarthy, Todd. "Samuel Fuller Brings in Par's Thriller 'White Dog' on Sked," *Variety,* June 19, 1981.
Moullet, Luc. "Sam Fuller sur les brisees de Marlowe," *Cahiers du Cinéma* 93 (March 1959).
Sarris, Andrew. "Fuller Up," *The Village Voice,* Jan. 17, 1984.
_____. "Samuel Fuller," in *The American Cinema,* Dutton, New York, 1968.
Selznick, Daniel. "An Old Pro on the Go Again," *New York Times Magazine,* May 4, 1980.

Works by Fuller

Books (Listed Chronologically)

Burn, Baby, Burn!, Phoenix Press, New York, 1935.
Test Tube Baby, William Godwin, New York, 1936.
Make Up and Kiss, William Godwin, New York, 1938.
The Dark Page, Duell, Sloan & Pearce, New York, 1944.
The Naked Kiss, Belmont, New York, 1964.
Crown of India, Award, New York, 1966.
144 Piccadilly, Baron, New York, 1971; New English Library, London, 1972.
Dead Pigeon on Beethoven Street, Pyramid, New York, 1974.
The Big Red One, Bantam, New York, 1980.
La Grande Melee, Christian Bourgois, Paris, 1984; as *Quint's World,* Worldwide, Don Mills, Ontario, 1988.
Pecos Bill and the Soho Kid, Bayard, 1986.

Articles (Listed Chronologically)

"What Is a Film?," *Cinema,* July 1964. (Republished in *Hollywood Directors 1941–76,* Richard Kozarski, editor, Oxford, New York, 1977).
"'Dead Pigeon' Livens Up Munich with Many 'Firsts' in Filming," *Daily Variety 39th Anniversary Edition,* Oct. 1972.
"News That's Fit to Film," *American Film,* Oct. 1975.
"War That's Fit to Shoot," *American Film,* Nov. 1976.
Contributor to *Bad Dates,* by Carole Markin, Citadel, New York, 1990. Fuller's comic vignette involves a blind date with "a squad of beautiful starlets."

Index